BABY'S FIRST YEAR FOR NEW PARENTS

BABY'S
FIRST YEAR
for New Parents

A Practical Guide for Taking Care of Baby and You

JAIMIE ZAKI

ROCKRIDGE
PRESS

Interior and Cover Designer: Irene Vandervoort
Art Producer: Janice Ackerman
Editor: Mo Mozuch
Production Editor: Nora Milman
Production Manager: Martin Worthington

All illustrations used under license from iStock.

Author Photo: Courtesy of Jaimie Zaki.

Paperback ISBN: 978-1-64876-481-3
eBook ISBN: 978-1-63807-284-3

R0

To my four Little Bears: Aiden, Camden, Amelia, and Kolbe. Thank you for teaching me so much about myself and this world.

Contents

Introduction

In 2014, I became pregnant for the first time. Like any new parent in the 21st century, I spent hours googling all my questions about pregnancy. Although pregnancy was a general mystery for me, I thought that because I was a nurse I knew all there was to know about birthing, breastfeeding, and caring for babies. Boy was I wrong! Becoming a mother was a whole new experience that I was *not* ready for.

I ended up having some scary experiences during my pregnancy, a traumatic birth experience, and a very challenging postpartum. For me and my husband, becoming parents did not feel like the beautiful miracle we had anticipated. The excitement was overshadowed by fear, stress, anxiety, and, of course, sleeplessness, which amplified everything. In the moment, we felt lost and couldn't help wondering, "What is wrong with us and what is wrong with our baby?"

The truth is *nothing* was wrong with us. The "problem" was the poor support systems in place for new parents. Health care providers who lacked compassion, doctors who lacked an ability to provide real support, a society that perpetuated myths that contradicted our every instinct, and no one to prepare us for what we were about to face. One doctor brushed off my very legitimate concerns as "nervous new parent" issues and not "real" issues.

We deserved better. Our baby deserved better. You deserve better.

This is why I've made it my mission to improve and expand support for new parents from pregnancy through the first year of your child's life.

Because we are a military family, our mothers were not close by to swoop in and save the day with grandma magic, but thankfully, I soon found La Leche League, a worldwide peer support group for breastfeeding mothers, and they provided me with the information, resources, and compassionate support I desperately needed. This group of mothers taught me how to find answers and use my voice. And that's exactly what I did. I learned that our feeding challenges were due to a tongue tie (see FAQ on page 140) in my infant, and this affected every other parenting challenge. When I addressed it with our pediatrician and lactation consultant, they told me I was *wrong* and should just *give up* on breastfeeding. But they didn't know I don't *just give up*. I'm a stubborn redhead who needed help and I was going to find it. Finally my mother came to visit and helped me hone my self-advocacy skills to get the answers we needed. And that's what we did. We drove eight hours to find a doctor to help us.

Once we fixed the tongue tie, feeding improved and so did life. I was able to begin finding confidence as a mother and I was inspired to teach other parents how to advocate for themselves and their babies. By the time my son turned one, I decided to become a La Leche League leader and worked toward becoming a certified breastfeeding specialist, then ultimately an IBCLC (international board certified lactation consultant). I trained to become a birth doula and postpartum doula so that I would have the expertise to support families from pregnancy through the postpartum period. As I write this, I'm nursing my fourth baby, reminiscing on how motherhood has completely transformed me and the path my life has taken. It's my distinct honor to walk alongside you as you embark on the journey to welcome your new baby and also meet a new version of yourself. You may hear me say, "little bear" or "baby bear" throughout the book. That's the endearing term we call our little crew and it's my dorky way of being cutesy to remind you that your little one is truly precious, not *just* a terrifying ticking time bomb of tears and poop.

To be honest, nothing can completely prepare you for welcoming your baby, but we can try! The most important skills to learn as a parent aren't diapering or feeding or learning how to function without sleep; they are self-advocacy and adaptability. This book is meant to be a starting place for you to dive in and learn more. It will equip you with a strong base knowledge so you don't feel like you're flying blind, and if you hit a roadblock you'll know when and how to advocate for more or better support.

PART ONE

An Introduction to Parenting

Preparing to welcome a baby looks different for everyone. But one thing is certain: It doesn't matter what crib you buy or what color you paint the nursery; what you really need to prepare is your heart, mind, and soul. In this part of the book we are going to talk about how to be prepared. We will explore common emotions and challenges that new parents face in the first year.

Throughout this section, I'm going to give you a prompt to help you process your thoughts and feelings. Let's start by chatting about what to expect when welcoming your baby bear. You can simply reflect on these prompts, chat with your support system about your thoughts, or use a journal or notebook to write down your thoughts.

REFLECTION PROMPT: *Before you get started reading, take a moment to write out your fears and concerns about welcoming your baby. What questions do you have? How do you expect to feel? How do you hope to feel?*

CHAPTER 1

Parenthood 101

Becoming a parent is scary. Whether this is your biological baby, adopted baby, or foster baby, you have been entrusted with this little person and that's a big deal. In a few years you'll look back and say, "the baby stage was the easiest," but right now it's uncharted territory. You don't have to navigate it alone. Before we get into the nitty-gritty of diapers, feeding, sleep routines, and so on, we need to explore the emotional side of parenting, especially during the initial transition. Becoming a parent is the purest expression of self-sacrificing love, but that can leave you feeling depleted and stressed. We will talk about how important your support system is, things you can do to prepare your heart for the changes to come, and what to do when the sleep deprivation sets in and you begin to feel like you aren't yourself anymore.

It's normal to experience negative feelings during this transition, but if you feel overwhelming, intrusive thoughts of self-harm or harming others, do not be afraid to seek a referral from your health care provider. Feelings of depression, anxiety, and rage are common and **you are not alone**, but intrusive thoughts of this nature are not healthy. Exploring talk therapy and other treatment options for potential postpartum depression, anxiety, and rage can be a crucial piece in improving your experience as a new parent.

Welcome to the Wild Ride of Parenthood

One rule to live by as a parent: Be flexible. This is easier said than done for most. Learning to expect the unexpected, roll with the punches, and take life one day at a time is essential. But it helps to have some kind of guide as to what is "normal" (is anything in life really *normal*?).

I always tell parents that the minute they "figure it out," *it* will change again. And that *is normal*. As a parent, you'll feel a roller coaster of emotions. And that *is normal*. Parenting will challenge and change you and your relationships with your significant other, your own parents, your siblings, and your friends, and that *is normal*.

What Does It Mean to Be a New Parent?

Welcoming your little bear is so exciting, but it can also be scary. Having a baby will impact and change your whole world. You will be required to adjust to someone else's schedule for feeding and sleeping and working and everything in between. Thankfully, we all know love is both the most powerful weapon and drug in the world, and becoming a parent usually comes with the biggest dose of love you've ever experienced. So if you're hopped up on love, that can only mean you'll figure it all out one way or another.

On that note, as far as the conversation on "normal" and "love" goes, I want you to know it is common to not necessarily feel overwhelming love for your baby immediately. Depending on your personality type, you may need days or weeks or even months to adjust before the overwhelming love feeling kicks in. That's okay. You'll still figure it out. I promise.

All different personality types become parents. And most of the time, partners have different personality types, which makes parenting even more complex. For instance, I'm a control freak and my husband is much more laid-back. How we perceive certain challenges is very different, therefore how we react is different. Our needs as parents are unique and that's true for you, too. Keep that in mind as you read this book and eventually encounter the world of *sanctimommies*. One tip I learned as a La Leche League Leader rings true still: As far as advice goes, take what works for you and leave the rest, whether that's my advice or Karen-at-the-grocery-store's opinion. Not all advice will apply to your life and worldview, and that's okay.

REFLECTION PROMPT: *How do you think your personality strengths and weaknesses will impact your parenting? How do you think your partner's personality strengths and weaknesses will impact their parenting? I encourage you to discuss this with your partner.*

Parenting a Baby in Our Modern World

Wondering what a *sanctimmommy* is? It's that mom on social media that is holier than thou and judges every other parent for making decisions differently than she would. There is a pressure to know it all, do it all, and be it all. These stressors, on top of the already well-known challenges of hormonal shifts, relationship tensions, and work-life balance really do make being a parent in the 21st century uniquely difficult.

Information Overload

The Internet truly is a blessing and a curse. Wading through online forums and blogs and scientific research to figure out what is accurate, safe, or simply what resonates with you can be overwhelming. It is important to find the balance of getting informed and being sucked into a black hole of contradictory advice.

Before your baby arrives, find a few trusted support people to consult with your questions and concerns. You can include both friends/family and professionals in this small circle. You can write down these names in your journal.

Check In with How You Are Feeling

Make sure to check in with yourself and your partner about how you're adjusting to all the changes that come with a new baby. Work together to brainstorm how you can help each other ensure that your needs are met despite working tirelessly to meet baby's every need. Postpartum depression is not unique to mothers, so it is vital that if either you or your partner find yourselves struggling, you support each other in seeking additional support. You can find more information on postpartum support in the Resources section in the back of this book (page 146).

Endless Comparisons

From Pinterest nurseries to Insta-influencers, we live in a visual world where everyone is comparing their lowest moments to others' highlights reel. The constant comparison can really contribute to the "not enough" feeling that many parents experience from time to time.

If you are particularly sensitive to the trap of comparison, I recommend limiting your social media time. Most smartphones have the ability to set app limits so you can minimize your time on Facebook, Instagram, etc. and focus more time on yourself, your family, and your baby.

The Pressure to Be the "Best"

When you're comparing yourself to others all the time, there can be a strong pressure to be the "best"—whether that's the mom who "bounced back" the best, or whose kid walked first, or whatever else. This can lead to real stress that can be draining and have a negative impact on your self-worth, relationships, and even bonding with baby.

When you're feeling inadequate, that's a sign you need some self-care. Share your feelings with your partner and make sure you're taking care of you: Eat nutritious meals and get exercise, plenty of water, and lots of rest, but most important, give yourself grace. If you're unable to practice basic self-care, then it's time to advocate for some help so you can get the break you need.

All You Can Do Is Your Best

So often, I work with parents who are crying because they learn something new and "wish they knew that before." And I tell them exactly what I'll tell you: You make the best decision you can with the information you have. There will always be hard decisions, something you're unaware of, and someone doing it "better" to make you feel inadequate. As long as you are making decisions from a place of love, you're doing your best. And if you learn that something was "wrong," that's okay! When you *know better*, you can *do better*.

Be Gentle with Yourself

When I was struggling with feeding my firstborn, I remember crying in the shower, convinced that if I couldn't feed my baby then I must be a failure, and he'd be better off with new parents. Do you know how ridiculous that is?

Unfortunately, many parents go through the same feelings. Give. Yourself. Grace. In fact, write that on a piece of paper and post it somewhere you'll see it every day. If you're facing a challenge, work toward a solution. Do not let that challenge own you. That's easier said than done, I know. But lean on your support system and remember that this baby was entrusted to *you*, and *no one* can love your baby better than you can.

Trust Your Parental Instincts

Just like no one can love your baby better than you, no one can care for your baby better than you. You know your baby better than anyone else. And this is a truth I remind my clients of regularly when I'm doing a home visit for lactation or postpartum support.

If you have a concern and feel like no one is listening to you, this is the time to practice those advocacy skills we talked about before. There's an acronym we recommend for medical decision-making during birth, but it applies to all decision making: BRAIN. This stands for Benefits, Risks, Alternatives, Intuition, Now/Never (what happens if we act now, never, or wait and watch?). This tool for thinking can help you advocate for you and your baby.

If you bring a concern to your health care provider and don't feel like they are taking you seriously, feel empowered to get a second opinion. Do not succumb to some ridiculous notion that you owe your doctors any loyalty if they are not listening to you.

Ask for Help

The first weeks of parenting can feel like a total blur. I look back on the first weeks of having a baby the same way I look back on a party night in college . . . glimpses of good, bad, and a whole lot of what the *bleep*?! But there's one thing college me did better than new mom me: Lean on my girlfriends for support.

Do not be ashamed of needing help. Most cultures have deeply held rituals during the postpartum period geared toward supporting the new mother. Unfortunately, Western culture doesn't seem to be on the same page. There's even less support for new dads.

You can start small. Invite friends and family to send a pre-made meal or take-out gift card to lighten the burden of daily cooking.

Above All, Enjoy Your New Baby

By now you're probably thinking, *This new parent thing sounds miserable!* I promise it's not all bad! Take in the snuggles. Relish that new baby scent. Brush your cheek against that soft baby hair. And don't forget to watch your baby's face as they sleep in your arms . . . that's when they make the most adorable little faces!

5-MINUTE MINDFULNESS FOR FEELING OVERWHELMED: *When you're feeling overwhelmed, I want you to lay down your baby somewhere safe, step outside in the sunshine, and breathe in fresh air. Repeat this phrase: "I am [baby's name]'s [mother/ father/your role] and I am good enough for them. This is hard but we will get through it together."*

Parenting Gets More Manageable with Practice

When my husband and I were first-time parents, we would look at other couples with more kids and think, *HOW are they surviving?!* Now, here we are, six years later with a total of four kids wondering how on Earth *we* are surviving. The funny part? The baby is the easy one!

As the days go by and you figure out rhythms and routines, you, too, will become a parenting pro! And as your baby grows you'll come to find each new stage brings new challenges, but you'll be more equipped to navigate them.

This Book Will Show You How

Knowing how to navigate challenges takes a little bit of base knowledge and a whole lot of skill. Remember, self-advocacy and adaptability are the top two skills you'll need on this journey. These skills come with practice. As for the knowledge part? I've got you. I'm going to share all my "entry-level" parenting tips so that you know when and how to employ the skills of self-advocacy or adaptability.

Conclusion

I know this whole parenting thing seems really overwhelming right now. And I know it can be scary when someone tells you that the only way to survive is to adapt and overcome, but you were made for this. If you weren't, you wouldn't be reading this book right now. Do not let this first chapter scare you! Fear is the opposite of confidence, and you are going to be confident.

REFLECTION PROMPT: *How can you shift your perspective to approach your fears and concerns productively?*

CHAPTER 2

Preparing for Your Baby

Preparing to welcome your baby looks different for everyone. When you think of preparing for baby, you may imagine a lavish baby shower, putting together a nursery, and maybe even taking all the childbirth classes the local hospital has to offer. Time after time, I see parents dreaming of all these things, then stopping hard and realizing that they have no idea what their baby *actually* needs versus what the marketing says they need. What use is it to buy all the best gadgets if your baby never uses them? Is the $2,000 bassinet really going to help you be a better mom or dad? Spoiler alert! All a baby really needs is you. Your baby needs you to love them and for you to be levelheaded because they have no clue what's going on in this world yet. Let's chat more specifically about all the changes soon to come.

Preparing for Your Baby Will Help You Adjust to the Change

There are a million and one books written about "what to expect" when you are welcoming a new baby. But the one thing you absolutely must expect: the unexpected.

I expected breastfeeding to be easy and "natural" and didn't think I needed to prepare much.

I expected that I would "sleep when baby sleeps" and be as energetic as always.

I expected that my baby would follow a very specific eating and sleeping schedule.

I expected a lot of other things and learned to adjust my expectations . . . and that lesson has followed me through motherhood as I parent toddlers and young children.

Take the expectations as a guideline, but remember that there are many variations of normal, and, as we discussed before, and I'll remind you again: Parenting is not one-size-fits-all, babies are not one-size-fits-all. There are, however, some things that you can pretty reliably anticipate: Your baby will constantly grow and change . . . but how? And how will you manage those changes? Let's learn more!

Here's What to Expect during Baby's First Year

By now you may have noticed I don't totally love the word *expect*, but it's catchy. However, let's call it "look forward to" from now on. When you're "expecting" something to happen, you can find yourself growing anxious when it doesn't happen exactly when you thought it would. However, when you're looking forward to something, you have a sense of joyful eagerness. *Looking forward to* your baby's milestones can help you feel excited without as much pressure and worry. What can you *look forward to* in the first year?

You can look forward to wishing your baby would sleep more, only to stay awake staring at him making sure he's still breathing. You can look forward to having your baby all figured out one day and then be totally clueless the next. Let's take a quick sneak peek at what these changes look like over the first year!

0–3 Months

We call the period between birth and 12 weeks old "the fourth trimester" because your baby will still be fully, biologically dependent on you. Babies in this stage seek maternal comforts that mimic the womb: constant warmth and safety (snuggles), constant food (cluster feeding), and even the sound of a beating heart (more snuggles . . . and sometimes sound machines). This is also a major period of adjustment for new parents where you will learn the importance of setting healthy boundaries with yourself, your partner, your family, and your friends, while somehow also learning to accept support from the same people.

3–6 Months

Whew! The fourth trimester is OVER! I'm finally starting to get the hang of this "parenting" thing. By now you may feel more confident that feeding is going well, routines have been established, and you understand your baby's little language.

Now that your baby has head control, they are all about exploring the world. This is a really fun stage, but all that curiosity can lead to sleep and feeding disruptions.

In the nature of exploring the world, your little one may learn how to sit unassisted and begin scooting or even crawling during this stage. Babyproofing the house becomes a priority.

6–9 Months

When babies hit six months, they become more independent and are constantly on the move. During this stage your baby may begin teething (if they haven't already), eating solid foods, and becoming even more physically active. Babies in this stage are learning to crawl and pull up, and some overachievers may even take their first steps. As you witness your baby's growth and development during this period, you may feel very excited. Keep in mind that the combination of physical and intellectual development, as well as teething, can lead to changes in feeding, sleeping, and behavior patterns.

9–12 Months

You're likely to feel much more confident as a parent by now and may start wondering, "what's next?" During this phase you may experience:

- Baby's first words

- More independence from baby: walking, running, climbing, and more

- Separation anxiety—Your baby may experience the "stranger danger" phenomenon, even with trusted family members or friends. This may even begin to cause a version of separation anxiety for you as well. We will talk more about how to manage this in chapter 8.

- Thoughts about weaning if you're breastfeeding

Every Baby Develops at Their Own Pace

Although some babies hit milestones "on time," your baby may not. You may find that your baby begins talking before others but starts walking after others. Just like we need not compare our lives as parents, we must try not to compare our babies to others, even their own siblings! Odds are, your baby will be walking, talking, and sleeping through the night before they graduate college.

It can be a challenge to know the difference between when something is really wrong and when you're feeling new parent anxiety. The safest bet is to talk to your pediatrician about milestone concerns during routine visits, and try to relax in the meantime. A lot can change in a few weeks or a few months.

There Are a Multitude of Ways to Prepare before Baby Comes

Preparing for baby looks different for everyone. Some will have everything "ready" before baby is born, while others will still have unfinished drywall in the nursery when mom's water breaks. Remember that the most important thing your baby *needs* is you. After that, it's about making sure your home has some basics to make life easier for everyone.

Make Sure Your Home Is Comfortable and Safe

Comfort and safety are the top two goals for any home. Although a newborn has fewer material needs than an older baby, here are some basic tips on ensuring that your house is a home for your little bear:

- Do not put blankets, stuffed animals, or bumpers on the baby's crib. Although these may seem comfortable, they're not safe. (We will discuss this more when we talk about safe sleep.)

- As your child becomes mobile, make sure to cover outlets, secure furniture to the wall, lock cabinets, and block off stairs or dangerous rooms.

- Never leave baby unattended around pets. It may help to bring home a baby blanket or onesie while they're still in the hospital so your pets can get familiar with their scent.

Figure Out Who You Can Ask for Help

During prenatal consults, I always recommend that parents create a list of 5 to 10 people they can call when they need support. This list should include family, friends, and professionals. Before your baby arrives, talk to your network about how they are willing to support you and when. Not everyone has that strong of a support system, but there are still people there for you! Look to your local hospital for new parent support groups, La Leche League for peer breastfeeding support, and consider postpartum doulas, night nurses, and lactation consultants available in your area.

Find a Pediatrician or Family Doctor (and Any Additional Medical Support)

One of the first places parents take their babies is to the pediatrician. I remember when my first was born, it felt like we lived there! Weight checks multiple times a week, and with my second, bilirubin checks multiple times a week. Finding a doctor you trust is extremely important.

Thankfully, most practices welcome new parent interviews. Some things you may want to discuss are how they may support your feeding choices, vaccination decisions, and how they'll manage after-hours concerns. It's okay to shop around to find someone who supports your family's needs.

It's Also Important to Take Care of You before Baby Arrives

I remember complaining about how tired I was when I was pregnant and someone telling me that I'd be even more tired after the baby was born. I'm happy to report that was false! Newborn tired is a whole new kind of tired, but I don't think it's any worse than other kinds of tired, and I still firmly believe pregnancy tired is the worst kind of tired, but maybe that's just me. That said, taking care of yourself physically before baby arrives is so important. Quality rest and nutrition are vital for strength and energy in the first days of newborn-world. Don't squander the opportunity to rest by staying up late getting the nursery ready! I promise it's more important for you to be rested. You need to be of sound mind going into the early newborn days. Going into it sleep-deprived and unfocused is doing no one any favors (trust me on that one).

Rest When You Can

You've probably heard it before: *Sleep when baby sleeps*. It's so true but feels so impractical. When baby sleeps you'll want to complete the laundry list—of well...laundry—that you're falling behind on, or you may just want some baby-free time to hang out with your partner. Here's my recommendation: Sleep when baby sleeps 70 percent of the time, and use the other 30 percent of quiet time for self-care, but do NOT overexert yourself with checking off your to-do list. If you *must*, prioritize one task per day, and spend the other baby-free time on self-care.

Resist the Urge to Compare Your Parenting Journey

When you're exhausted and your baby is screaming incessantly, it's easy to wonder why they aren't as calm as your cousin's baby and beat yourself up for not brushing your hair in a week when your sister always looked so put together . . . just stop. Everyone's needs, priorities, and struggles are different and you won't see them all.

I know I'm saying, "Stop comparing yourself" over and over, but it's because in this world you need that constant reminder. So I'm going to keep reminding you: You are unique, your baby is unique, and your journey is unique.

Fake It till Ya Make It

Speaking of writing things on the mirror, I recommend coming up with three to four mantras or affirmations for parenting. Just like people swear by "birth affirmations" to stay focused in labor, I believe that repeating uplifting affirmations and practicing spiritual rituals has transformed me as a mother and I believe it can do the same for you. Write out inspiring quotes, scriptures, or prayers and post them around your house. You may not feel confident just yet, but the more you encourage yourself, the more your confidence will take root and begin to bloom. Here are a few favorites:

- "I am the best parent for my baby."

- "This, too, shall pass."

- "I'm going to miss this. I don't think I will, but I will."

- "These are the 'good old days.'"

Conclusion

Parenting really is a roller-coaster ride. Sometimes you have it all figured out and the next day, you're right back at square one. Fortunately, things are guaranteed to change on this journey—when you least expect it. Remind yourself that nothing lasts forever and that you'll figure it all out eventually. Keep that reminder handy—write it on a mirror or on a sticky note. Savor the good as much as you can. Your little bear will be a very big bear before you know it, and you'll miss the snuggles and adventures of today.

PART TWO

Spit-Up, Diapers, and Tears, Oh My!

In this section of the book we will dive into the nitty-gritty how-to of parenting, from feeding and diaper changes, to learning your baby's unique little language. Many of these basic skills seem daunting now, but we'll start with baby steps and in a few months, you'll be a pro!

CHAPTER 3

Bringing Your Baby Home

C ongratulations! You're finally home with your little snuggle-bear! You and your baby will probably both shed some serious tears . . . but you'll learn that the love of family is stronger than any other force in this world. In this chapter you will learn some skills needed to survive the early days of baby!

Welcome, Baby!

Can you believe it? This little person you've been preparing for the last nine months (or longer) is finally here! I remember thinking that I was so ready to welcome my first baby, and then when it happened for real, I felt like I was thrown to the wolves and told to fend them off with a spoon.

I was so happy to have my little guy home with me, and I loved snuggling him, but to be honest, I wasn't very fond of him. I didn't like him, and I certainly wasn't sure I *loved* him, yet I knew I'd gladly defend him with my life. You may experience something similar. I want you know that these first days are hard. Your whole world has been turned upside down. You need to give yourself grace. I know what you're thinking: *How will I actually survive?* Keep reading and you'll find out!

The First Few Weeks Will Fly By

I always regret feeling so overwhelmed in the beginning because those days go by so fast that it seems like a blur looking back. Four babies in and I always approach the first week with an expectation of endless exhaustion, but I blink and there's a full-grown child running around. Everyone says, "You'll miss it when it's gone" and it sounds cliché and dismissive of the challenges . . . but in a way, it's true. This is your time for bonding and connecting. Nothing in life worth having is easy and the same is said for parenting. But I encourage you to step back and find the beauty.

REFLECTION PROMPT: *If you get a few minutes of quiet after baby goes to bed for the night, I want you to get a journal and list three moments that warmed your heart. Write down what happened, and how it made you feel. Come back and read about these moments on days where you are overwhelmed, crying, and wondering what that "joy" thing looks like.*

Prioritize Sleeping, Eating, and Getting to Know Each Other

You have two jobs right now: Take care of yourself and baby.

You need to focus on eating, sleeping, and bonding with baby. Laundry and other chaos can wait. One reason new parents feel overwhelmed is because they feel this weight of having to "do it all." They have to keep baby alive and stay on top of housework, work responsibilities, and whatever else . . . but it's not true. You *need* to take this time. Ask family or friends to pitch in around the house or drop off food. Look for professionals to help you tidy up or handle your laundry.

The Importance of Connecting with Your Baby

Connecting with your baby is crucial. Research shows that well-adjusted children are those with a healthy attachment to their parents. These children go on to develop healthy interpersonal and romantic relationships later in life, perform better in school and at work, and are better able to cope with life stress.

This attachment starts at birth. Secure attachment from day one can give your baby a leg up on life. Unfortunately, connecting with your baby may not always come naturally. Welcoming a baby you adopted or who was born via surrogacy can present unique bonding challenges. Even modern birthing practices, such as separation at birth, and social demands on parents in the newborn stage often hinder the natural bonding process.

Thankfully, even if it feels like the world is against you, there are some wonderful ways you can start facilitating attachment early, despite the challenges you've faced.

Strengthen Your Bond

Sometimes the biological process of parent-infant bonding is interrupted. Many parents find that they need to facilitate their bond with their baby by taking more time to form an intentional connection. You are not alone! Thankfully, by utilizing responsive parenting and attachment parenting techniques, you can begin facilitating these bonds immediately.

Show Love and Affection

You know that "baby voice" people tend to inexplicably default to when talking to their baby? That's a form of love and affection. Even when we're not feeling it fully, our instincts are to show our babies love. We are responsive. We answer their cries, we use playful tones to soothe them, and we snuggle them until they settle down. Even though we may think they don't understand the little "I love yous" whispered during naps, those loving actions and tones lay down neurological pathways in the brain to create a foundation for connection.

It's Good for Your Baby's Development

Responsive parenting and attachment parenting styles are vital for your baby's development. A baby who grows up without healthy attachment is often stuck in "fight-or-flight" mode and less likely to hit milestones on time or develop healthy communication skills and tools. This can actually affect their long-term outcomes regarding performance in school, workplace, and even personal relationships down the road.

Did you know ... physical contact and connection is so important to your baby's health that without it babies can actually become sick? Simply being well-fed is not all your baby needs to stay alive and healthy—your baby needs YOU and YOUR LOVE.

REFLECTION PROMPT: *This is a great time to think of your relationship with your own parents and consider things you want to pass down and things you want to do differently. Talk with your partner about how you plan to bond as a family as well.*

How to Pick Up the Baby

Babies are not as fragile as they look! I remember the first time I held my baby, I was sure I'd drop him. After four babies of my own and working with countless newborns, picking up a baby is second nature for me now. But I can always see that glimmer of fear in a new parent's eye as I casually pick up their baby without a fear of breaking them. I've even had dads tell me they're amazed how I casually handle a baby because they feel like they're handling a grenade. With time and practice, though, they all build their confidence.

Be sure to always support baby's neck and keep close contact. Pick up your baby by using both of your hands and grab baby around the chest/under the armpits with your thumbs on baby's chest and fingers on their back, supporting the neck. Bring your baby close to your body for the desired holding position.

How to Hold the Baby

There is no right or wrong way to hold a baby. What is important is that you are supporting baby's neck and securely enough to control the squirm. Using pillows when you sit and baby carriers when walking around can help safely support your baby.

CRADLE HOLD: This is the classic baby hold you think of when you envision a swaddled newborn. Support baby's neck and head in the bend of your elbow with your free hand providing extra support on baby's bottom.

UPRIGHT: This is how you'll instinctively hold baby when burping them, but a lot of babies enjoy chilling out in this position as well. Put baby's belly against your chest, with their head on your shoulder with one hand on baby's bottom and the other hand on baby's upper back.

MAGIC BABY HOLD: This is the one that resets your screaming baby 9 out of 10 times. Using your dominant hand, hold baby's belly against your forearm, your hand supporting baby's chin/head, legs straddling your elbow. Use your other hand for stabilizing support/to pat baby's back. Swaying in this position can help reset your baby.

How to Swaddle the Baby

When most people think of a baby, one of the must-have skills that comes to mind is swaddling . . . and no one ever seems to know how to do it quite like the labor and delivery nurse.

The truth is, you don't have to be a good swaddler. Baby should be spending most of their time skin to skin with parents, and being swaddled too frequently can limit baby's range of motion and make it harder to express early feeding cues and practice motor skills. That said, swaddling is totally an amazing tool to utilize in moderation. Need to go to the bathroom without listening to your baby scream? Use swaddling to trick them into thinking they're still being held tight. Here are some common swaddle techniques you can use.

The Receiving Blanket

1. Using a large receiving blanket (I recommend muslin blankets), make a triangle with the point toward your body and the folded edge away.

2. Lay baby with feet toward the point and neck on the folded edge.

3. Tightly pull the left point across baby, tucking arms in, and tucking the blanket behind baby's right side a bit.

4. Now pull the bottom point up to baby's right side and tuck.

5. Finally, pull the right point toward the left and wrap around baby's back.

6. Rock your baby burrito!

The Swaddle Blanket

1. Buy a hook & loop swaddle blanket.

2. Tuck baby's legs into the pocket.

3. Cross the left side over their body and secure the hook & loop.

4. Cross the right side over their body and secure the hook & loop.

When Should You Stop Swaddling?

If you are bed-sharing with your baby, do *not* utilize a swaddle for bedtime. This is dangerous because it can cause baby to overheat. Additionally, it limits baby's motor communication, which can be an important part of safe bed-sharing. Taking away your baby's ability to bat a loose blanket off their face or kick at Mom and Dad to signal a need puts your baby in danger.

Furthermore, once your baby has the ability to roll over, you need to stop swaddling. Swaddling past this stage can create a risk of entanglement. This would be a good time to transition to utilizing a sleep sack kind of product.

How to Burp a Baby

After feeding, it's common for baby to ingest some air and therefore need to burp. If your baby is getting restless during or after a feed, or even crying, that is a sign they may need to be burped.

Traditional Burping Method

1. Hold baby upright in nondominant arm with baby's belly to your own chest/shoulder.

2. Use dominant hand to pat baby's back.

3. Add in a light bounce.

Sitting Up in Your Lap

1. Hold baby upright on your lap facing your nondominant side.

2. Use your nondominant hand to support baby's chin/head.

3. Use dominant hand to pat baby's back.

Keep in mind that not all babies need to be regularly burped. Bottle-fed babies and breastfed babies with a poor latch are more likely to get air during feeds and need frequent burping. If your baby grows exceptionally fussy during a feeding, you could pause to try burping.

Understanding Your Baby's Needs

Within a few days of getting to know your baby, you will learn their language. When your baby is hungry, they will display certain behaviors that are different than when they're tired or needs a diaper change. The more you play with and get to know your baby, the better you'll be at understanding them. I used to cry along with my babies asking, "What are you trying to tell me?!" and now I can tell my husband exactly what's wrong when I hear the baby start crying in the other room. It's an amazing transformation and you will get there with time.

What Do Their Cries Signal?

Being born without the ability to speak does not mean they do not have the ability to communicate. Crying is one of their primary communication tools. Crying doesn't always indicate sadness, fear, or pain. Sometimes crying means your baby simply wants attention. Other times crying is a signal that something isn't right. After a while you may notice that your baby utilizes a different pitch of cry in different circumstances.

HUNGER

Everyone's first thought when a baby cries is that they must be hungry. But did you know that crying is actually the last feeding cue your baby will give? Although we will learn more about feeding cues later on, it's important to understand that if your baby is crying to signal hunger that they are very hungry, they may have a hard time settling down to eat, so this cry may sound very frantic and desperate.

DIAPER CHANGE

If your baby is well-fed and crying, one cause may be the need for a fresh diaper. Sitting in a dirty diaper is uncomfortable and you can be sure that your baby will let you know! If your baby develops diaper rashes, they may cry more dramatically, indicating they are experiencing extra discomfort. Keep ointments and powders on hand just in case.

Have you ever been so tired you can't sleep? It sucks. Babies can become overstimulated quite easily and experience this feeling as well. They will sometimes fight sleep and startle just as they begin to fall asleep. Usually, all they need is some extra cuddles!

How Can I Comfort Them?

Fussy babies are typically seeking what I call "maternal comforts": motions and sounds that mimic the conditions of the womb. Of course "on the outside," anyone can help provide these comforts. *Remember the Four S's: shush, swaddle, sway, suck.*

Shushing mimics the sounds of blood pumping through the mother's body. Swaying is soothing like the motions felt in the womb as the mother would walk, dance, or sway. Swaddling can be very comforting to a little one who isn't being actively snuggled. And of course, babies have a natural need for sucking. This includes both feeding and *non-nutritive* sucking. The magic baby hold we talked about earlier in this chapter (page 27) incorporates many of these tricks to help soothe your baby almost instantly.

Have Patience with Yourself

Being a new parent is stressful. It can be hard to cope with the 90,000 tasks and appointments we need to keep straight, being screamed at by a baby you don't understand, all while running on no sleep and wondering if your partner is as overwhelmed as you or thinks you're crazy because you two truly haven't bonded with each other in weeks. Whew. It's. A. Lot. And you're going to find balance. You will learn what works for you and what doesn't. You just need to give it time.

You Will Learn as You Go

I always laugh at how hard we say our first baby was and how easy the subsequent babies have been. I think the transition was just harder with the first because we didn't know what we were doing. As we trudged through the first months, we learned so much about each other and ourselves. Once we learned how to advocate for ourselves and baby, things started to feel much less overwhelming. You'll find your groove, too.

YOUR BABY WILL LEARN, TOO

Babies are literally learning from INSIDE THE WOMB. Babies pick up on routines quickly and you may be surprised how they learn to become a part of your life. Include your baby in your routines instead of centering your routines around your baby. This will allow your baby to integrate to the family. *Just remember to stay flexible.*

REFLECTION PROMPT: *Use your journal to record what challenges you most as a parent each day and brainstorm three solutions (they can be totally reasonable or completely absurd). Look back at the end of the month. I bet you'll be surprised to see just how much you overcame and learned in a short amount of time.*

Conclusion

Learning how to include your baby in your daily life, overcome the overwhelming stressors of worry and fear, make sure you're keeping your baby safe and healthy, while also meeting your own needs and those of your other family members can be really challenging. But with time and practice you and your baby will become pros at this surviving thing . . . and before you know it you may just be thriving, too. It takes time to establish a routine and then more time to get into a groove that works for the entire family.

CHAPTER 4

Feeding Your Baby

You'll often hear people say, "fed is best" but the truth is, fed is minimum. The bare-minimum requirement for keeping your baby alive is feeding them. Somehow infant feeding has become a topic of much debate and drama in our culture. There is an entire industry based on perpetuating myths about infant feeding. There is a lack of quality information available, and no one can ever seem to provide unbiased support for parents' feeding choices. In this chapter I will help you learn about the basics of infant feeding so that you can make a well-informed choice to meet your family's needs, regardless of your situation.

Babies Eat ... a Lot!

In the early days it can feel like your baby wants to eat 24/7. This can lead to a lot of stress because parents are unsure if their baby is eating enough. It's very important to understand that babies eat a lot. And to be honest, it never stops! Toddlers through teenagers ... growing kids need tons of fuel. Still, it's important to understand what is biologically normal for a baby's nutritional requirements, so let's explore some common questions new parents ask all the time.

How Often Will My Baby Need to Eat?

I'm sure you've heard of putting your baby on a feeding schedule. Some people say babies need to eat every two hours, while others say every three or four. I want you to wash that idea out of your head right now. Strict feeding schedules are frustrating for parents, babies struggle to gain weight, and milk supplies are negatively impacted. Instead, practicing on demand feeding allows you to be a responsive parent and makes for healthier, more content babies.

Babies and their needs change so frequently throughout the first year. As an advocate of responsive parenting, I highly encourage you to establish feeding routines based your own baby's needs. These are the patterns we typically observe as infants grow:

FOURTH TRIMESTER: Babies cue to feed about 8 to 12 times over 24 hours; cluster feeding is common.

3–6 MONTHS: Babies may space out feedings. However, distracted feeding can cause more frequent but shorter feeding sessions. Either can be a normal variation of changes in your baby's feeding habits.

6–12 MONTHS: Around six months, you will introduce solid foods to your baby. Solid food plus breast milk or formula may cause changes in your child's eating patterns and routines. It is important to ensure that milk is still your baby's primary source of nutrition.

Are There Physical Signs that My Baby Is Eating Too Much or Too Little?

You can tell your baby is getting enough milk by monitoring weight gain trends and stool and urine output.

- Initial weight loss up to 10% is normal.

- Your baby should have one poop and one pee diaper per day of life for the first week (day three should have three pees and three poops).

- After the first week, we expect about five to six pee-and-poop diapers per day. If your baby goes more than 24 hours without stooling, call your pediatrician ASAP.

- We expect babies to be back to birth weight by two weeks old, and to then continue on their own growth curve. Percentiles do not matter unless they begin dropping percentiles. This is a sign you may need feeding support.

Deciding How to Feed Your Baby Can Be Complicated

There are many debates about breastfeeding versus bottle-feeding. You have many options. You can feed at breast, pump breast milk, feed donor milk, or feed formula. Between the modern-day stressors on families, societal expectations, and myths perpetuated about infant feeding, it can be hard to make decisions about infant feeding. It can be especially hard if you're making a decision that is different than how your family members have fed their babies, because that can have an impact on support. For instance, being the first in the family to breastfeed can be hard when no one in your family has ever breastfed and cannot offer experiential support. Likewise, choosing not to breastfeed when you come from a very pro-breast family can feel uncomfortable and isolating. Things to consider when choosing how to feed your baby include:

- Biological benefits of breast milk compared to formula

- Health considerations your baby may have (the only health condition that truly excludes breast milk as an option is galactosemia; most other medical conditions encourage breast milk as optimal nutrition)

- Financial commitment and budgeting

- Support systems at home, work, and school

- Medical conditions in the mother

- What does feeding on the go look like?

- What does feeding look like after returning to work?

Why Parents Choose Breast Milk

Breast milk is the biologically anticipated food source for your infant. Breast milk is unique in that it is a live substance that is always changing to meet your baby's individual needs. For premature babies, breast milk is extremely important because it reduces the risks of necrotizing enterocolitis (NEC), a deadly condition seen in NICU (newborn intensive care unit) babies. Colostrum, the very first milk your body makes for your baby, is considered vital for newborns because it is packed full of antibodies and helps properly colonize the gut microbiome. Infants who are breast milk–fed have a lower risk of long-term health concerns such as allergies, asthma, type 2 diabetes, and other chronic health conditions than their formula-fed counterparts. Breastfed infants also tend to have a healthier gut microbiome. This doesn't even begin to mention the benefits to bonding, establishing attachment, ease of multitasking/feeding on the go (once you get used to breastfeeding and find your groove), and the fact that breast milk is usually much more cost-effective than formula.

Common Challenges

Although breastfeeding comes with many benefits for both parents and baby, there are many challenges that come along with breastfeeding. Taking a breastfeeding course prenatally can help you prepare for many of these challenges in advance, and possibly even prevent other challenges altogether. Common challenges breastfeeding parents may experience include:

- Discomfort in the early days as you learn to latch your baby properly

- Engorged breasts and leaking milk

- Challenges getting a deep latch, causing sore nipples

- Slow weight gain

- Feeling "touched out"

- Navigating pumping with feeding

- Lack of support from employers/educational institutions

- Perceptions of judgment from family, in the workplace, and in public

- Poor support from trusted sources (i.e., OBGYN, pediatrician) who do not have adequate breastfeeding training

Supplies You'll Need

In a perfect world, the only "supplies" you need for breast-feeding are a baby and breasts. That's it. And for many dyads, that's all that's needed (plus a little support). But there is other "breastfeeding gear" you may find yourself using:

☐ Nipple creams

☐ Warm/cold packs

☐ Breast pumps and bottles

☐ Milk collectors

☐ Supplemental nursing system, nipple shields, and syringes*

☐ Breastfeeding pillows

*I recommend using these tools only after consulting with an IBCLC once you are home from the hospital.

Supporting Your Milk with Your Diet

Some of the most googled questions about breastfeeding are: "What should I eat to make more milk?", "What food should I avoid when breastfeeding?", and any variation related to these questions. Here's the deal: You do not need to eat anything special. Breastfeeding does demand about 300 to 500 extra calories, so you may find that you need to increase your own caloric intake to ensure your own nutritional needs are being met. I highly recommend eating a well-rounded, diverse diet to ensure that you are maintaining adequate levels of key nutrients for your body's stores. Your body will deplete your nutrient stores to feed your baby, so eat nutrient-dense meals and keep taking your prenatal vitamin.

Why Parents Choose Formula

There are many reasons why parents choose to formula-feed their babies. For some, it is as simple as they were never exposed to breastfeeding, so they're just not comfortable with it. For others, they would love to breastfeed but medical conditions make that impossible. And for yet others, there's a critical lack of support that makes breastfeeding feel too overwhelming. Sometimes breastfeeding parents need to combination feed with formula to increase their infant's caloric intake for a myriad of medical reasons. Adoptive parents may choose to formula-feed because other options such as inducing lactation or using donor milk are simply impractical to incorporate into their lifestyle. Whatever your reasons are for using formula, it's a decision you probably aren't making lightly and you should feel respected and supported. Meeting your baby's needs is the priority here.

Common Challenges

Although there are plenty of pros to formula-feeding your baby, the challenges formula-feeding parents face are different than those breastfeeding families face; however, they can be just as emotional to endure:

- Extra dishes to handle

- Formula is expensive, especially if your baby requires hypoallergenic or other specialty formulas

- Packing for travel and even simple errands requires extra gear to make sure formula is available when needed

- Safe preparation can be misunderstood and even inaccessible in some locations and during states of emergency (for example, power outages and water outages)

- Feelings of judgment from others who chose not to formula-feed

- Sense of loss if formula was the solution for a challenging breastfeeding experience

Supplies You'll Need

- ☐ Clean bottles and nipples

- ☐ Access to clean water that can be boiled

- ☐ Formula that is recommended by your pediatrician

- ☐ A cooler for outings

- ☐ A bottle warmer for outings

Why Parents Choose Bottle-Feeding

Sometimes parents deeply value the benefits of human milk but are uncomfortable with breastfeeding or struggle with a baby who cannot latch effectively. These parents often choose to "exclusively pump" for their babies or offer donated breast milk via bottle. Anticipated separations such as work, school, or business trips are other reasons why parents may choose to incorporate bottle-feeding expressed breast milk into their baby's feeding routine. Some consider this the best of both worlds although others consider it the worst. Me personally? I think anyone so dedicated to their baby that they choose to pump breast milk all day, every day—for days, months, or years—is a superhero.

Common Challenges

- Pumping enough milk to fully feed your baby expressed milk can be exhausting physically, logistically, and emotionally.

- You need space and time for bottle and breast-milk storage, preparation, and cleanup.

- Power outages and unexpected appliance failures can be stressful and detrimental to a milk stash.

- You need to bring extra gear for outings to keep milk chilled and safe for consumption.

- It can be emotionally demanding, especially if your pumping routine interrupts your sleeping routine.

Supplies You'll Need

- ☐ Bottles, nipples, milk storage bags

- ☐ A pump (double electric, ideally), flanges, extra pump parts

- ☐ Pumping bra and other breast pumping accessories

- ☐ Nipple creams to reduce friction with pump

- ☐ Coolers for outings

- ☐ Freezer space at home (if you have an oversupply of milk; not everyone has a large breast-milk stash, and that's totally normal and okay)

How to Breastfeed

Recognizing early feeding cues and feeding on demand is optimal for supporting milk supply and practicing responsive parenting. These include:

- Stirring from sleep

- Smacking/licking lips

- Rooting reflex

- Bringing hands to mouth/chewing and sucking on hands

- Whimpering and whining

- Crying

Note: If baby is screaming/crying, attempt to calm before feeding. This is a late-feeding cue and baby is extremely hungry. They will struggle to latch while upset and begin associating breastfeeds with being upset and very hungry. Calming baby allows them to latch more effectively and associate breastfeeding with calm.

As you may have heard, the key to comfortable breastfeeding is achieving a "good latch," but what does that mean?

- Wide mouth—corner of infant's mouth forms an obtuse angle

- Flared lips—top and bottom lips are flared out, not tucked under

- Includes nipple *and* areola

- No pain (as you and baby learn to breastfeed together, discomfort at the beginning of feed is normal if it goes away; pain lasting the duration of feed is not normal)

The key to achieving a deep latch lies in *proper positioning*. There are multiple positions that are conducive to achieving a comfortable latch. But there are a few things that all positions should have in common:

- Ensure that baby is "tummy to tummy" (or tummy to side in a position like holding a football).

- Make sure that baby has proper alignment (ear, shoulders, and hips should form a straight line). Make sure baby's head is not turned to one side.

- Be certain that infant's chin is extended, not tucked.

- Use a "sandwich" or "C" hold on the breast with one hand and support your baby's head and neck with the other hand. Doing this helps compress the breast almost like squeezing a giant hamburger before eating, making it easier for baby to achieve a deep latch.

- Tap the nipple to your baby's top lip; this will encourage baby to open wide.

- Allow baby to self-attach. If baby struggles to get a deep latch, unlatch and try again, rolling the breast/nipple into baby's mouth. It is not necessary to smoosh baby to the breast.

- Do not settle for a shallow/painful latch—seek help from an IBCLC if you're having a hard time.

Once your baby is latched, let them nurse on the first breast until completion (entrée breast), then offer the second breast (dessert breast). The next feeding session start with the breast you left off with: The dessert breast will become the entrée, and the entrée will become dessert.

Note: Feeding logs can be helpful, especially if you are having breastfeeding challenges; however, do not feel like you must prioritize tracking feedings if your baby is healthy and breastfeeding is going well.

How to Bottle-Feed with Breast Milk

Bottle-feeding is not one-size-fits-all, and your baby may need specific adaptations depending on why you are bottle-feeding. Please be sure to consult with your IBCLC for creating a bottle-feeding care plan unique to you and your baby. These are common guidelines for bottle-feeding breast milk to your baby:

- Use a clean bottle and nipple (sanitizing is not necessary for healthy, full-term infants, but may be advised for NICU babies).

- Choose a nipple with the slowest possible flow.

- Practice paced feeding 3 to 4 ounces of milk.

  ▶ Hold baby in an upright position.

  ▶ Keep the bottle parallel to the ground.

  ▶ Tap the bottle to baby's lip, encouraging self-attachment.

  ▶ Encourage a wide, deep latch similar to breast latching.

  ▶ Allow baby to work for milk and set the pace for the feeding, take breaks as needed, and do not rush feeding.

SAFE MILK STORAGE GUIDELINES

FRESH EXPRESSED, ROOM TEMP	61–79°F	4–8 HOURS	THE WARMER THE ROOM IS, THE LESS TIME MILK SHOULD STAY OUT
Fresh in refrigerator	32–39°F	3–8 days	Ideal to store in back of the refrigerator, avoid storing milk in doors; check for signs of spoilage before freezing or using.
Refrigerator, thawed	32–39°F	24 hours	If there are ice crystals in the milk bag, milk can be refrozen; do not refreeze completely thawed milk.
Freezer as part of a refrigerator	Less than 39°F	3–6 months	Store toward back, avoid storing in doors.
Deep freezer	About 0°F	6–12 months	

Other Tips for Safe Storage:

- Date milk when storing.
- Freeze flat in a plastic bag to save space.
- Freeze in 1 to 4 oz. portions to minimize milk waste (most bottles you prepare for your baby will be 2 to 4 oz.).
- Combining expressed milk can be done safely.

- Thaw milk slowly in the refrigerator or hold under running water; start with cool water, gradually warming until the bag is thawed.

- A warm water bath can warm expressed milk—NEVER microwave expressed breast milk. Doing so will heat the milk unevenly, which can cause cold pockets and hot pockets that can scald baby.

- Cooled milk will separate; this is normal. Stir or shake milk to recombine for feeding. (There are myths that breast milk should not be shaken. You are not likely to damage milk by shaking to mix; however, it may create frothiness from air bubbles.)

Sometimes a breastfed baby does not want to take a bottle from another caregiver; this is normal and can take time. You have many options for ensuring that your baby is fed during separation.

- Be consistent with offering the bottle when mom is not nearby.

- Offer bottle for fun with no pressure when baby is not ravenous.

- Utilize a bottle-feeding alternative (cup feeding, syringe feeding).

- Caregiver could wrap baby in one of mom's worn garments that smells like her.

- Learn about reverse cycling (sometimes it's okay if baby refuses a bottle during separations).

- Work with an IBCLC to create a personalized feeding care plan.

How to Bottle-Feed with Formula

For the most part, guidelines for formula and breast-milk bottle-feeding are pretty similar. Even a baby who is not breastfed should follow paced feeding guidelines.

- Use a clean bottle and nipple (sanitizing is not necessary for healthy, full-term infants, but may be advised for NICU babies).

- Choose a nipple with the slowest possible flow.

- Mix formula carefully, following the directions to ensure proper ratios. Too much or too little formula-to-water ratio can make a baby extremely ill.

- Use boiling water to prepare formula. Formula is often contaminated with a variety of microbes. Boiling water kills these microbes.

- Allow formula to cool to a safe temperature for baby. If you batch-mix formula and keep it in the refrigerator, your baby may prefer the milk slightly warmed. Place bottle in a pot or bowl of warm-hot water and allow it to warm up.

- Practice paced feeding.

  - Hold baby in upright position.

  - Keep the bottle parallel to the ground.

  - Tap the bottle to baby's lip encouraging self-attachment.

  - Encourage a wide, deep latch similar to breast latching.

  - Allow baby to work for milk and set the pace for the feeding, take breaks as needed, and do not rush feeding.

Knowing When to Wean Your Baby

Weaning is a controversial subject. Some consider weaning to be the introduction of non-breast milk or formula supplementary foods. Others consider it the stage when baby starts to breastfeed less. The World Health Organization and American Academy of Pediatrics both support breastfeeding beyond a year, and even longer than two years if desired. If breastfeeding is no longer mutually desired, weaning should begin. Sometimes weaning is necessary for certain medical reasons as well (although it is rare for an infant to have a medical indication to wean). There are many approaches to weaning. Here are some tips:

- Don't ask, don't offer

  ▸ If baby doesn't request milk, you don't offer it. You also don't deny requests. This is a slower approach to weaning.

- Redirection

  ▸ When baby requests nursing, you redirect to a different activity, substitute snack/drink before providing a nursing session. This is another slow approach.

- Limit length of nursing session

  ▸ Tell your baby that "milkies go bye-bye" when you're done singing a song, saying a rhyme, etc.

  ▸ I used to let my daughter nurse and then start a countdown from five. After a few days of introducing this boundary, she learned to unlatch on the count of one. As I decided to proceed with weaning, this made it easier to gradually make feedings shorter and shorter without protest.

- Cold turkey

  - ▶ Sometimes parents have to quit breastfeeding cold turkey. It's not an easy approach but it is an option. It's good to have another person available to help soothe baby and give mom a break from the emotional toll this approach can take on both mom and baby.

When Do I Start Solid Foods?

According to the American Academy of Pediatrics (AAP), the human infant's diet should be exclusively breast milk or infant formula until around six months, at which time complementary foods can be offered. The AAP and World Health Organization emphasize that breast milk or formula should be the primary source of baby's nutrition for the first year. Solid foods can be introduced at six months old if your baby is displaying all of the signs of readiness. These include:

- Ability to sit unassisted—this is crucial.

- Developed palmar and pincer grasps (self-feeding can help further develop pincer grasp)

- Ability to grab food and bring to mouth

- Loss of tongue thrust reflex

- Interest in food (Being interested in food and putting stuff in their mouths alone does not indicate readiness! Babies explore everything with their mouths from an early age. The other developmental milestones must be met as well.)

Supplies You'll Need

Baby feeding supplies really depend on if you plan to utilize the baby-led weaning method or not. Truly, you just need a safe place for baby to sit and some food, but common supplies include:

- Safe highchair
- Eating utensils
- Cup of water
- Bib
- Floor mat for ease of cleanup

At the end of the day, introducing solid foods can be as intricate or minimalist as you desire.

How to Introduce Solid Foods

Many parents are advised to begin introducing solids with baby cereals. This is actually outdated advice. Many of the often-quoted reasons for introducing baby cereal are not actually evidence-based. Furthermore, baby cereals are simply calorie bombs that offer very little nutrition. If you do choose to start with a baby cereal, please be very cautious and *do not* feed it via bottle because it can create a choking hazard.

Parents will often purchase prepackaged baby foods that are pureed blends of fruits and veggies, moving their baby to the next stage as they grow. Baby food stages become chunkier and less pureed with each stage. There have been recent concerns, however, with the safety of prepackaged baby foods containing dangerously high levels of heavy metals. For this reason, some parents choose to make their own pureed baby foods from scratch at home, which is quite simple with a blender or immersion blender.

The other option that is growing in popularity, and my personal favorite, is baby-led weaning.

Allergies and Choking Hazards

When introducing solids, parents are often concerned about what foods are safe and what to avoid. In general, the only food that must be avoided is honey before the age of one year old. Otherwise, pretty much anything is fair game! Even high-risk allergens such as peanut products, eggs, etc. should be introduced early (around 6 months) because studies show that earlier exposure reduces risk of allergy development whereas waiting (the old school recommendation) increases allergy risk. Other foods that you may want to avoid are foods like popcorn and nuts because they can be choking hazards. Snacks like grapes and hot dogs should be cut into very small (not round) pieces to prevent choking.

Letting Baby Take the Lead

Baby-led weaning (BLW) is an approach to solids where you let baby take the lead. This method makes feeding not just about forcing yucky foods, but exploring and learning. Babies are offered the same foods the rest of the family is eating (within reason) and are encouraged to explore textures, colors, and tastes. BLW can be messy and slow, but it provides an opportunity for your baby to learn and develop optimally. BLW is like teaching your baby to walk before running. They learn to explore the food and chew it before learning to swallow, and they naturally desensitize their gag reflex at their own pace, so BLW actually decreases choking risks.

An important note for BLW: Gagging is noisy, choking is quiet. Although your baby should always be supervised during feeding to prevent choking, be aware that gagging, although it sounds scary, prevents choking. If you haven't taken a baby CPR class, I would recommend doing so before introducing solids so that you know how to handle a choking infant if the situation should occur.

Use Feeding as a Time to Bond with Your Baby

Feeding is about more than food. It's about relationships and bonding. Dinner dates are a very common way of getting to know a new romantic interest, friend, or business partner. Parties and celebrations are often centered around food. Food is about more than just food in our world. And that's true for babies, too.

Breastfeeding, specifically, is not just about food. It's about comfort. It's about communicating. It's about bonding and connecting. This can be achieved with bottle-feeding, too. Feeding times are an ideal time to meet your baby's need for eye contact and social interactions with you.

Conclusion

I know it can be very overwhelming to learn about all your options, especially when it comes to feeding. Feeding your baby can feel really huge and complicated because it is so important. But truly, a few years from now, no matter how you feed your baby, your toddler will decide to eat some gross three-day-old food they find tucked in their car seat.

CHAPTER 5

Putting Your Baby to Sleep

As adults, our sleep habits are dictated more by society than biology, so adjusting to our baby's biological sleep patterns can be extremely challenging. Understanding the ways we, as humans, are actually wired can help us understand the changes in sleep patterns that come with early parenthood. This understanding means that we can approach sleep challenges with plans instead of panic. It is my wish that this chapter will help you understand your baby's needs so you can meet them with grace.

Babies Sleep . . . A Lot!

It's normal for a newborn to sleep up to 20 hours a day. TWENTY HOURS!! So why are we so dang tired? Of course, that time is split into tiny segments of sleep around the clock with no solid 8-hour stretch like we are accustomed to, so *that's* why we're so tired. Sleep is vital for the rapid development our little ones experience, yet throughout the first year of life infant sleep patterns change a lot. Let's learn more about what we can expect and why it's happening.

Sleep Is Important for Your Baby's Brain

Have you ever watched a baby sleep? They make some of the funniest faces. This is because their brain processes EVERY-THING they've learned throughout the wake times, including facial expressions. One of my children would even practice crawling in his sleep. I'd wake up to find him absolutely asleep but on all fours, rocking back and forth! During developmental leaps (like mental growth spurts), you'll find that your baby sleeps a lot more. When they come out of "the sleepy stage," you'll notice they're like a new little person. You can see their brains working differently as they learn and practice new skills.

How Often Do Babies Sleep? How Much Sleep Do They Get?

Although every baby is a little different, this is how much you can expect your baby to sleep in the first year. These are totals within 24 hours, and will be broken into naps that typically last 1 to 2 hours, and ideally at least one 5-hour stretch. (Did you know 5 hours is considered "sleeping through the night"?)

- Newborn: 16–20 hours of sleep

- 3–6 months old: around 15 hours of sleep

- 6–12 months old: around 14 hours of sleep

How Does Sleep Shift During Year One?

As you can see, throughout the first year your baby will sleep less and less. However, their sleep patterns often become more defined and predictable. Typically, by four months you will see that your baby has a "morning nap" and "afternoon nap" type of routine during the day. Overnight, you may see that your baby tends to sleep a total of 8 to 10 hours; however, this block of sleep tends to be broken up with one or two wake-ups. Sometimes their routines will shift for the following reasons: illness, developmental growth spurt, teething, major life transitions (for example, parent returning to work, travel, starting daycare, etc.).

Make Sleep Safety a Priority

Safe sleep during the first year is extremely important. Every parent's biggest fear is putting their baby to sleep and then they never wake up. Although SIDS is a huge fear, a preventable threat is suffocation/entanglement during sleep. This is why it is recommended to avoid items such as blankets, anything with strings, crib bumpers, pillows, and stuffed animals. An empty crib is a safe crib.

In addition to cribs, other safe sleeping environments include bed-sharing, room-sharing, and bassinets. There are benefits and risks to all sleep locations. For instance, some parents are worried about bed-sharing because of suffocation risk, yet research has shown that safe bed-sharing poses no increased risk for SIDS. On the flip side, sleeping alone in a crib has been shown to reduce suffocation risk, but increases SIDS risk. Some decide that a good middle ground is room-sharing but not bed-sharing. Regardless of where you choose to put your baby to sleep, it is crucial that you take steps to reduce risks.

Preventing SIDS

Sudden infant death syndrome (SIDS) is every parent's worst nightmare. There seems to be so much information and not enough all at the same time. SIDS is often an unexplained phenomenon and differs from suffocation, though the two are frequently lumped together. Although there are many theories on what causes SIDS, researchers are still not 100 percent sure of the cause. Thankfully, there are some precautions parents can take to prevent the risk of SIDS.

- Breastfeeding
- Co-sleeping
  - ▶ Room-sharing with baby in parent's room in a crib or bassinet for the first 6 to 12 months
  - ▶ Bed-sharing: Follow Dr. McKenna's "Safe Sleep Seven" guidelines. Here's a song from La Leche League International to help you remember: (to the tune of "Row, Row, Row Your Boat") *No smoke, sober mom/ Baby at your breast/Healthy baby on their back/ Keep them lightly dressed./Not too soft a bed/Watch the cords and gaps/Keep the covers off their head/For your nights and naps.*
- Pacifier use—the sucking is believed to help prevent SIDS, but if your child doesn't take a pacifier, don't fret about it. Most babies spit them out, anyway.
- Back sleeping can prevent getting into too deep of a sleep; however, once baby can roll independently, belly sleeping is considered safe.
- Being in a nonsmoking home.

Key Safety Tips for Baby Sleep

Although there are options for safe sleep locations including cribs, pack and plays, bassinets, and even parents' beds (under certain circumstances), there are some places babies should never be left to sleep.

- Car seat—napping in the car seat in the car or stroller is okay because of the angle of the car seat, but on the floor (or washing machine or countertop where some parents place their baby seats) puts the seat at an angle that doesn't support an open airway.

- Swings, vibrating chairs, soft-sided baby "docks" or "nests" and other devices are usually not designed for safe, unsupervised sleep. Once baby is fast asleep, it's safer to gently move them to their crib.

- Couches, recliners, futons, beds with gaps between the frame or wall

Establishing Your Family's Bedtime Routine

It's really important to establish routines with infants. Although strict schedules can set up most people for extra stress, a routine helps create healthy and predictable habits. Before your baby is even born, you can start with your own healthy habits like dimming the lights at a certain time, unplugging from screens (TV, computer, phone, etc.) at least a half-hour before bed, and incorporating personal hygiene practices. When your baby arrives, you'll be able to ease them into your routines slowly.

What's Best for Sleep Training?

There are countless methods of sleep training. A popular technique known as graduated extinction, aka "cry it out," is the subject of much debate. This technique involves letting your baby cry for several minutes on their own before going in to offer comfort in order to acclimate them to falling asleep and waking alone. When parents are desperate for sleep and nothing seems to be working, "cry it out" and "controlled crying" methods of sleep training can be very tempting. There is research supporting this method as safe and effective, and there are arguments against it as well. So, what is a parent to do? Responsive parenting sounds great in theory but sleep deprivation is a serious issue and needs to be dealt with safely. How do you do that? **Respond to your baby's needs as well as your own.** Shift your own habits and routines to promote healthier sleep patterns and opportunities for rest.

How Do Naps Fit In?

Often babies seem to be confused about when to sleep. Newborns may sleep for long stretches during the day and be up all night. A week or so of ensuring nighttime sleep happens in the dark and day naps happen in well-lit rooms should cure this. As your baby grows, you can expect to see your baby set a pattern of having a morning nap and afternoon nap. With older babies who require less sleep, it is advised that the afternoon nap end about five hours before bedtime to ensure sleepiness at bedtime.

Managing Sleep Regressions

Many parents describe developmental phases where sleep patterns shift as "sleep regressions." The truth is that sleep is not linear. "Sleeping through the night" is not a milestone that is achieved and lasts forever, as you may know based on your own sleeping patterns.

Sleep is very closely related to brain development, and during major shifts you may find that your baby has a harder time falling or staying asleep. This can be extremely challenging and stressful for parents. My best advice to coping with these changes is to maintain routines but be responsive to your baby. For example, if your baby typically sleeps well from 8 p.m. through 1 a.m. but has shifted to waking up screaming every night this week at 10 p.m., go to your baby, provide comfort, but do not turn on bright lights, play, or utilize screens because these activities will stimulate your baby and create unhealthy sleep associations. Instead, use a dim light (dimmable salt lamps are great for this) and nurse your baby, break out that magic baby hold, or implement whatever other special tricks you've discovered to help your baby through their discomfort. Remind yourself why your baby is experiencing these changes and that it won't last forever.

Sleep When Your Baby Sleeps

I've said it before, and I'm saying it again. Sleep. When. Baby. Sleeps. As often as you can. Towels can wait to be folded. There will be times when you can't sleep when baby sleeps . . . especially if there are other children to care for. That's okay! Just try to use that time to rest. My personal rule of thumb is to use morning naps as an opportunity to catch up on life and use the afternoon nap as a rest time for myself. Then when baby sleeps at night, catch some z's. When 2 a.m. rolls around, you'll be glad you took that weird nap at 7 p.m.

Common Sleep Problems and How to Solve Them

The most common complaint parents have about sleep is night waking. This is a protective mechanism against SIDS. But beyond that, do you ever have a hard time sleeping because of changes in your life? Do you ever wake up to use the bathroom? How about getting a sip of water or indulging in an occasional midnight snack? Have you ever just woken up at night simply "because" and felt oddly refreshed just to see it's only 1 o'clock in the morning?

Babies are human, too, and have the same needs, only they can't fulfill them on their own. Keep the lights low, respond to your baby's need, and go back to sleep. If both of you getting sleep means you bring baby into your bed, that's okay! Just remember those safe sleep rules.

Your Baby's Sleep Ritual Is a Great Time to Connect with Them

I want you to think about how you sleep best. A lot of people will express that they experience their best night of sleep after caring for their bodies and their souls. What I mean is, many people find they sleep best after they've nurtured their souls with some reading, music, meditation/prayer, and connecting with their loved ones. I know personally I sleep best if I know my husband is next to me. Babies are no different! They need connection, especially after busy days where they may have become overstimulated. Bedtime routines are a great time to connect with your baby with focused attention and physical touch. This is why rocking or nursing your baby to sleep is *not* a bad habit. Many people will discourage sleep nursing, but it can be a great opportunity for you and your baby to feel connected and can make bedtime easier for your baby.

Conclusion

I hope that this chapter has helped you see that sleep is important and can be stressful, but when you understand you and your baby's needs and learn to work with them, you'll be able to survive, and maybe even thrive. A few things that tend to help babies sleep better is a bath and clean diaper. So, let's hop on over to the next chapter to learn about how you can keep your baby comfortable so you can all sleep better.

CHAPTER 6

Diaper Changes and Bath Time

Before becoming a parent, I worked for a while in long-term care facilities assisting the elderly. I was very familiar with poop . . . thinking about poop, keeping track of poop, talking about poop, cleaning poop. Yet I was still not quite prepared for dealing with baby poop (which, for the record, I prefer). In this chapter I will do my best to prepare you for the impending poopageddon.

Babies Poop . . . a Lot!

I remember when my son was about two weeks old. It was my husband's first Father's Day. We were at church, and I was rocking the baby and passed him to my husband. Not three seconds later my son pooped all over my husband and we had to leave church because it was such a mess. It's still our favorite poop story because we could not stop laughing that it was the perfect first Father's Day gift.

Over the years and among all our kids, we've had our fair share of poop explosions that left us asking, "*How* does this kid produce *this* much poop?!" But the funny thing is, each blowout is almost like a mini celebration at the same time. Although poop is gross, it's usually a great indicator of your baby's health status. So, we've always taken comfort in knowing that these massive poops were signs of healthy babies.

How Many Diaper Changes Should I Expect per Day?

During the first week of life, we expect babies to have one pee and one poop per day of life. So, on the third day, we expect to see three pees and three poops. Now, the pees are often combined with the poops. Any poop the size of a quarter or larger is considered adequate. After this, you can expect anywhere from three to six poops per day, although more can be normal, too. You'll notice during the first week that the poop changes colors from black meconium to a greenish transitional stool, then to a yellowish mustardy stool in breastfed babies. Formula-fed babies can have different poop colors and consistencies, often thicker, greener, and smellier than their breastfed counterparts. Do keep in mind that there is a wide range of "normal" when talking poop.

What Kind of Diaper Should I Use?

Parents ask which diapers hold up best. But they also have to weigh other factors like how sensitive baby's skin is to different brands, how expensive diapers are, how sustainably they're created, and how convenient they are when we are out and about. Who knew diapering had so many considerations?!

Disposable

Disposable diapers are a fairly modern invention. If you grew up like me, disposable diapers were one of the huge saviors of modern parenthood. Every big-box store has at least one aisle, if not more, dedicated to various brands and sizes of diapers with all kinds of cute names. But how do you know if they're actually the right choice for your family?

BENEFITS

- Disposable diapers can be bought almost anywhere.

- They are lightweight and easy to pack in a diaper bag.

- They fit well under clothes.

- They are easy to change and dispose of without much maintenance or care.

CHALLENGES

- Disposable diapers are typically made with lots of chemicals that can produce rashes, even from organic brands.

- Disposable diapers wreak havoc on the environment and spend decades in landfills.

- They can be expensive.

- They can be hard to find during emergencies and natural disasters when people are stocking up on essentials.

Cloth/Washable

As a child I remember my mom talking about cloth diapers as if they were an ancient relic. She talked about babysitting kids with cloth diapers and how they were such a hassle to care for. I was intrigued but put off after hearing my mom's stories, but when I was looking for a solution to blowouts, I found cloth diapers. I quickly learned that modern-day cloth diapers are no ancient relic! They work very similarly to disposable diapers, except they're cute and fluffy and reusable.

BENEFITS

- After the initial investment, they last years and can save a lot of money over multiple children.

- They are not made with the same chemicals as disposables, so may be better for sensitive skin.

- They reduce landfill waste.

- As long as you are able to do laundry, they never run out.

- They generally contain poop explosions much better than their disposable counterparts.

CHALLENGES

- Extra laundry! For some people this is significant, for others it's a barely noticeable increase in your normal laundry routine.

- Can be costly up front.

- Take up more space when packing for outings.

▶ Traveling can be challenging to pack cloth diapers and find convenient laundry facilities.

More about Cloth Diapers

Cloth diapers can be overwhelming to start because there are so many options. My favorite system includes pocket diapers with charcoal bamboo inserts for daytime and bamboo all-in-ones with a double gusset cover for overnight. However, what works for me may not work for you. There are tons of systems to choose from! If you're planning to cloth diaper, I recommend buying one to two diapers of each system and figuring out which you like best before investing in a whole stash of the same system. If the upfront cost is off-putting to you, see what you can find used. Many people keep their diapers in great condition, and you can sanitize them before use.

How to Change a Diaper

As an older sibling and former nurse, I find changing diapers to be second nature. But now the torch is being passed on and you must learn. Thankfully, it's not as hard as it looks. I have a special trick for making diaper changes seamless.

1. Gather supplies (fresh diaper, wipes).

2. Open the fresh diaper, place it under your little one's bottom (with the dirty diaper still on! This is crucial for a seamless diaper change!).

3. Lay 1 to 3 wipes within reach, already pulled out of the pack.

4. Open the dirty diaper and use the diaper itself to wipe front to back to remove the bulk of the "yuck."

5. Lift baby's bum by holding both ankles in your nondominant hand, fold the diaper in half (so that if you laid down your baby, the outside of the dirty diaper would be touching their back).

6. Wipe front to back as needed and lay dirty wipes on top of the dirty diaper (dirty-side down).

7. Still holding baby up, roll the dirty diaper up and move to the side.

8. Put baby back down on top of the clean diaper, then close the diaper.

9. Put the dirty diaper in the trash. (If using cloth diapers, rinse off soil if needed and place in a wet bag for laundering.)

Important Tips for Baby Boys

If your son is circumcised, it is important to make sure that the wound stays clean until it heals. If there is still foreskin remaining, as is often seen with a "loose circumcision," you may need to retract skin to ensure cleanliness and prevent adhesions.

If your son's penis is intact, it is very important to avoid retracting the foreskin. That can create abrasions and open him up to infection. It's also very painful! So, when cleaning an intact penis on an infant, you would clean it the same way you would your finger: base to tip.

Important Tips for Baby Girls

Girls are at a slightly higher risk for urinary tract infections if their diapers are not kept very clean. To help prevent UTIs in your baby girl, be sure to wipe front to back ALWAYS. Never wipe from the anus toward the vagina/urethra.

Sometimes you will notice poop inside the labia. Gently separate the labia and use a wipe to remove the soiling; however, it is not necessary to clean inside the vagina because it is a sphincter that will not allow poop to enter.

It can be normal in the early days for a breastfed baby girl to have some blood in her diaper. This is a hormonal reaction to birth and breastfeeding and can mimic menstruation. Although it seems alarming, in most cases it is completely normal. If there is a large amount of blood, consult with your provider.

Reading Your Baby's Diaper

Your baby's diaper can actually give you a very detailed picture of their health and well-being. As a lactation consultant, I ask for detailed descriptions of diaper output to help determine a baby's status. Diaper output can give a lot of insight to your baby's hydration status, fussiness, and more.

Healthy Urine

When evaluating normal urine, we look at frequency, volume, color, and odor. We've discussed frequency of diapers in newborns. In older infants we expect a minimum of six urine diapers daily. Sometimes it can be difficult to assess volume of urine, especially in combination with poop diapers. That's why many disposable diapers have a urine detection line on them. They can detect small volumes of moisture so that you can be certain that your child is urinating (especially in the early days when low-volume urines are common). Furthermore, we would expect healthy urine to be pale yellow and relatively odorless. Deviation from "normal" once in a while is to be expected; however, consistently abnormal urines could be a red flag.

Although healthy urine can indicate a healthy baby, there are urine characteristics that could serve as a red flag:

Blood—Blood present in the diaper could be normal; however, it could also be a sign of UTI. If your baby has blood in their urine, call your health care provider promptly.

Dark Urine—Although dark urine can be within the realm of normal, consistently dark urine, especially in low volumes accompanied with a foul odor, could be a sign of concern.

Brick Dust—Sometimes newborns will have uric acid crystals in their urine that are orange, pink, or reddish in color. If this happens once, it is likely within the realm of normal. If it happens consistently, it can be a sign of dehydration and need for medical attention.

Keep in mind that once or twice could be a variation of normal, but consistent presence of these red flags, especially in conjunction with other symptoms in your baby, can be a sign for urgent medical evaluation.

Healthy Stool

Did you know that poop comes in many colors?! Healthy stool means a healthy baby, but many people assume that colorful stool isn't healthy. In the first days you'll encounter a brownish black poop called meconium, but it will transition to a brownish green, then to a mustard yellow. Occasional green poops are not uncommon and can be a variation of normal. I've even seen blue poop before.

Although there are variations of normal, sometimes changes in poop can be the first sign of a health concern. If you ever have concerns, I recommend documenting with photos.

Occasionally you may even want to save the diaper to give to your provider for a stool sample.

- Green, mucous stool

  ▶ If this is your baby's norm and it is accompanied by discomfort or other symptoms, chat with a health care professional. It could be benign, or a sign of allergies and inflammation.

- Bloody stool

  ▶ Call your health care provider.

- Chalky white stool

  ▶ Call your health care provider or go to an urgent care/ emergency room.

- Loose stool/diarrhea

  ▶ It is normal for babies to have frequent poops, and especially for breastfed babies to have looser stools. Some babies poop every feeding, and then some. Typically, for babies, it is not considered diarrhea unless poops exceed 12 to 16 per 24 hours and/or accompany other symptoms of illness.

- No stool/constipation

  ▶ It can be considered common for a breastfed baby to go up to a week without stools. This is typically not a cause for concern, though it can be a sign of an off-balance gut microbiome and future constipation problems. If your baby is in pain and experiencing difficulty stooling, contact your provider because daily poops are ideal.

  ▶ Foul odors—poop stinks, especially when you introduce solid foods. But keep an eye out for exceptionally foul odors. Although rare, this can be a sign of intestinal infections such as *Clostridium difficile*. Call your provider with any concerns.

Dealing with Diaper Rash

When your baby is screaming inconsolably from a red tushy, there's a part of your heart that just breaks. Diaper rashes can seem to come out of nowhere and linger, leaving you feeling helpless and hopeless. Diaper rashes can be experienced at different levels of severity. Sometimes it's just some uncomfortable redness, other times the skin can look truly angry and even open up and bleed. Diaper rashes do not usually require a call to the pediatrician unless they are persistent or open and bleeding, which creates risk for infection.

There are many approaches to dealing with diaper rashes, so here are some tips:

- Keep diapers dry—the longer your baby sits in a soiled diaper, the higher the risk for skin breakdown.

- Change the brand of diaper or switch to cloth diapers. Sometimes diaper rashes are a result of reactions to chemicals in disposable diapers.

  - If you already use cloth diapers, be sure the diapers are being washed properly and all the laundry soap is rinsed out. Consider using a Free & Clear detergent to reduce risk of reaction.

- Use a quality diaper cream.

  - I usually recommend using a non-petroleum oil-based herbal cream featuring calendula and other gentle herbs that promote skin healing.

- Barrier creams are sometimes an important key to healing stubborn rashes. Zinc-based creams are a common option.

● Baby powders are popular for keeping diapers dry but there are things you need to consider.

  - Make sure you're using a talc-free powder for your baby because talcum powders have been linked to long-term health concerns like cancer.

  - Even talc-free powders can be dangerous if baby breathes in the particles, so be cautious not to accidentally create a "cloud" with the powder.

Common Skin Irritations and Treatments

Your baby may experience rashes or baby acne from a variety of things. Drool rash is very common, as drool is on their face and chin much of the time. Pacifier use, food particles, teething, and frequent face-wiping can also irritate baby's delicate skin. Detergents and perfumes may also irritate the skin. Use gentle soaps to keep the irritated area clean and use dye or chemical-free detergent. For dry areas caused by irritation, use a softening cream to add moisture to the area.

Newborn Skin Care Guide

When babies are born, they're usually covered in a white cheesy substance called vernix. Vernix is amazing for your baby's skin. Before I knew what vernix was, it looked like something yucky that needed to be immediately washed away. But I later learned it's actually amazing for your baby's microbiome, the well-balanced bacteria inside of us, *and* hydrating your baby's skin! Rubbing the vernix into babies' skin is healthier than you may have expected. This is also why it is recommended to wait to give your baby a bath, if possible, until they are at least a few days old.

Good bacteria are being colonized and bathing too soon could cause an imbalance, negatively impacting the microbiome. Furthermore, bathing lowers body temperature, which newborns typically struggle to maintain. Additionally, water and soaps are actually very dehydrating to newborn skin. That said, keeping skin clean in the early days is an important part of preventing rashes and yeast infections. Milk from feeding or spit-up can get trapped in rolls and skin folds, creating a prime environment for fungal growth and skin irritations. During the first week of life, I recommend using a sponge bath approach to keep the skin clean while avoiding dehydrating the skin too much.

How Many Baths Are Too Many?

There seems to be a fine line between too much bathing and not enough. Personally, I wait at least two weeks after birth for the first "real" bath. After that, we bathe our babies on an as-needed basis to keep their skin healthy. We do sponge baths most days to make sure rolls and folds are kept clean and dry but save "real" baths for when they're obviously dirty (for example, super sweaty, stinky, or after a diaper blowout). As your baby grows older, you may choose to do a daily bath as a part of the bedtime routine. Although daily bathing isn't typically necessary for humans of any age unless they are physically dirty, you can keep this evening water play healthy by not adding soaps to the bath except when necessary.

IF YOUR BABY STILL HAS THEIR UMBILICAL CORD . . .
Umbilical cords can fall off in the first few days of life or hang around for a week or more! This is one reason we do only sponge baths early on. Soaking the umbilical cord is not recommended, because you're trying to let it dry out to fall off.

How to Bathe Your Baby

When we first bathed my son I remember thinking, *I just figured out how to hold that wiggle worm without dropping it and now we're gonna go make him slippery with water and soap?!* Bathing babies can be very scary the first time. Odds are, you and your baby will both survive bath time! Did you know there is actually more than one approach to bathing your baby? My personal favorite is co-bathing. The easiest way for me to bathe the baby is to get in the bath, have my husband hand me the baby, ease baby into the water, laying them on my chest/belly and wipe them down. It feels like I have more control this way, and it's great for bonding as well. (In fact, as a lactation consultant, co-bathing is one thing I frequently recommend for non-latching babies to experience a limbic reset, or relaxing of the nervous system.)

Co-bathing isn't always a practical option, though, so more convenient options are using the sink or a baby tub.

1. Fill up the sink/baby tub about halfway with warm water. There are some cute rubber duckies on the market that change color to let you know if the water is too cold, too hot, or just right. In general, though, your baby will transition best to water close to body temperature (98 to 99°F).

2. Keep one hand on baby at all times! Dip feet in first, laying into the sink or tub in a reclining position. (If using a sink, I recommend a towel on the edge of the counter into the sink so baby's head can rest comfortably, if you are not using some kind of insert.) Water should come up to baby's mid-belly.

3. Use a washcloth to wipe down baby. I prefer to start with the face, move down the body to the feet, and end with the private parts and bottom. Don't forget to go between skin folds. (Soap is optional!)

4. If you used soap, be sure to rinse baby using a small cup.

5. Drain water, then swaddle baby in a hooded towel with the hood folded under.

6. Run sink water to a safe temperature, hold swaddled baby in one arm with their head over the sink (or have your partner hold baby while you wash).

7. Wet baby's hair and massage in shampoo with fingers or using a soft-bristled brush in a circular motion.

8. Rinse hair thoroughly, then use the hood of a towel to cover baby's head until dry.

9. Take baby to a bed or changing table to dry baby off (don't forget between the rolls!) and put on a clean diaper.

As your baby grows, this routine will change. They'll be able to sit up and splash around and you'll face new challenges. Anti-slip mats in the tub can be helpful for maintaining safety during baths.

Supplies You'll Need

As always, there are must-have and nice-to-have supplies. Bath time is no different! What do you need?

- Safe place to bathe baby (co-bathing, sink, or baby tub)
- A washcloth and towel
- A dedicated tub cup for rinsing
- Free & Clear soap (optional)
- Anti-slip mats for bigger babies
- Bath toys as baby grows
- Temperature-indicating toys or a water thermometer

What Shouldn't I Put in My Baby's Bath?

As we talk about what is safe during baths, you may be wondering if there is anything that should NOT be added to baths. I recommend never adding anything, except *maybe* Epsom salts, to a baby bath, especially during the early days when skin is more sensitive.

If you choose to use soap, I recommend putting it on a washcloth, not adding it directly to the bath water. I also encourage you to avoid bubble bath solutions for your infant. Aside from concerns about ingredients, bubbles are unnecessary for very little babies and can create a dangerous, slippery situation. You should also avoid bath oils of any kind, including essential oils.

Diaper Changes and Bath Time Can Be Fun for Parents and Baby

Anytime you are providing hygiene care for your baby, it is an opportunity to bond. To be honest, I dread bathing and diapering, so I outsource that to my husband whenever possible. He loves to use bath time and diaper time as fun time with baby. He makes up games and even songs! Now when a baby needs a diaper change, it's not uncommon to hear me sing, "Iiiittt's daddy-diaper-duty time, daddy-diaper-duty time" as I hand the baby off to him. He takes over singing and dancing with baby as he changes their diapers. Then he takes full advantage of the giggles and after the diaper is changed, typically spends the next few minutes playing giggle games.

Conclusion

By now you should be feeling prepared for the practical how-tos of parenthood! From feeding, to sleeping, to diapers, the basics have been covered. How are you feeling about finding and implementing routines that work for you? Here's a tip that works well for me:

Get some caddies from your local big-box store and use them to create feeding stations, diapering stations, and a bath box so you always have your "must-haves" within reach. It will make implementing your routines much easier.

Now that you're ready to deal with feeding, bathing, and pooping, let's get ready to take a deeper look at your baby's health and development throughout the first year.

CHAPTER 7

Your Baby's Health and Development

Your baby's health is your top priority as a new parent. You want to make sure you're doing everything you can to keep baby's physical and social development on track. So in this chapter we will explore what to expect from each stage of development to help you anticipate the major milestones. I do want you to keep in mind, however, that your baby will likely take their own path. If you have any concerns about your child's development, be sure to consult your health care provider. But you'll often find that no two babies are alike in their development (even twins!) and that having patience is half the battle.

Your Baby Will Grow and Change Every Day

We will go into more detail about milestones in chapter 9, but let's touch on how your little one will develop through the first year. Babies don't grow just physically; they mentally lay down new synapses, learn how to express their feelings and needs, how to explore the world around them, and how to interact socially with other humans. They are constantly learning and adapting. It's a lot! When your baby is born, let's be honest, they will probably seem kind of boring. Your little one will eat, sleep, and poop . . . but not much else. However, just a short 12 months later, they will be walking, talking, and feeding themselves?! The changes that occur during the first year are so fascinating and occur so rapidly, you better be careful not to blink!

Mentally

Behind baby's sleepy eyes is a magical world of brain development. Synapses (your baby's neurological base) are being laid with every sound, kiss of sunlight, and touch of the breeze. Every moment that passes, your child is developing memories that lay the foundation for how they will learn and grow in the future. Over the first year, your baby will blossom from a fully dependent little human to a much more independent child with a growing personality.

Emotionally

Emotional development in infants can be hard to understand. Because crying is their only mode of communication for so long, it can be easy to assume that little ones don't feel love, joy, sadness, etc. But the truth is, they're more than helpless, biologically driven beings. During your daily interactions, they witness your own expression of emotions and even experience them in their own minds. However, they have no clue how to control those emotions or even identify them. This can mean they experience emotion very dramatically. Infants can quickly go from maniacal laughter to a meltdown of frustration. Your job will be to help them learn to identify and regulate those complex and intense emotions.

Verbally

Did you know language begins developing in utero? Babies can actually hear spoken words in the womb and begin developing language skills that early! In the early days your baby will make those stereotypical cooing sounds that can be so fun. Be cautious not to get too caught up in using baby talk with your infant, however. Although mimicking sounds is great for teaching them language, it is also important to speak to them with dignity, using correct pronunciation and a normal tone so they can develop healthy verbal skills beyond baby talk.

Physically

We tend to focus on weight gain, height, and other physical signs that our baby is growing well, but remember that healthy babies come in all shapes and sizes. Did you know your baby's hair and even eyes may change color during the first year? Sometimes babies are born with blue eyes and by the time they reach their first birthday, they've changed to a different color (this is usually due to exposure to the sun and melanocyte development). Often the soft, wispy baby hair will gradually fall out and grow back in a different color or texture. These are other reminders that your baby, just like you, is always changing a little bit every day.

THROUGH MOVEMENT

When infants are born, they depend on reflexes to survive. The rooting and stepping reflex in combination helps them locate their mother's breast to feed. We sometimes see the startle reflex when there is a loud sound, and we see infants sucking on their hands to indicate hunger. But soon they begin to move more intentionally. Rolling and scooting can catch you off guard, and next thing you know, they're crawling, then running!

THROUGH THEIR SENSES

One of the most amazing things about babies is how they learn with every single sense they possess. Infants explore the world on their hands and knees, feeling every surface and texture, and even TASTING them! This stage of sensory play and exploration is crucial for creating a strong foundation upon which to build the rest of their experiences in the world.

Socially

Along with all these changes, your baby will change socially. This may be the most fun and heartwarming experience you'll witness. During the first few weeks of life, your newborn's idea of social engagement typically involves demanding milk and receiving it. Soon, your baby's gaze will turn into intentional eye contact with emotion connected to it. Sleepy smiles will turn into social smiles as they react to something silly you say or do. Before you know it, your baby waves hello and goodbye and intentionally seeks interaction by reaching for the people around them.

Supporting Your Baby's Development Is Key

We previously discussed the benefits of attachment parenting and how this approach can help support your baby's development by creating a sense of security (see page 25). Once your baby has developed a sense of trust in you, they are free to explore their world without hesitation or fear (not always a comforting concept as a parent!). It is crucial that you understand how simple day-to-day experiences and moments affect your child's development. You are the model your child will replicate.

0–3 Months

During the first three months of life your baby is still very much dependent, similar to life in the womb. Biologically driven, your child doesn't seem interested in participating in society quite yet. But this is a time when your child is truly soaking everything in. How you can help:

- Use black-and-white picture books and patterns to visually stimulate your baby's brain (they see best in black and white early on).

- Develop healthy attachment (see more on page 25).

- Mimic your baby's sounds and facial expressions.

- Engage in lots of tummy time by lying on the floor together and encouraging them to develop their neck and back muscles as they react to you.

Tummy time allows your infant to spend supervised time on their belly to develop strength and coordination skills. If your little one seems to despise tummy time on the floor, you can practice by starting it on your own body. Allowing baby to practice tummy time on your belly or on your legs can help them feel secure in this new, sometimes uncomfortable, position.

3–6 Months

This is a time of rapid development! Your child will begin rolling, scooting, sitting unassisted, and possibly even crawling. Your child will likely have developed an intentional palmar grasp (the ability to pick up items using their palms) and will learn to put everything in their mouth to fully experience it, whether that is an electrical cord or food or teethers. Be sure to keep a close eye on baby! They will surprise you with how quickly they incorporate a new skill into their daily activity.
How you can help:

- Increase tummy time.

- Lay baby on a safe surface with interesting toys just barely out of reach so they feel motivated to move toward the items.

- Sit with baby between your legs, using your body for support to allow them to practice sitting.

- Baby activity mats can be very fun for babies to explore.

6–9 Months

Six months old is a huge milestone! Your baby is now likely ready for table food and is beginning to experience life in a whole new way. Your baby is more social and may even be learning basic words like Mama and Dada.
How you can help:

- Repeat sounds your baby makes and speak clearly to encourage baby to repeat sounds you make.

- Use simple sign language (if you know it) whenever you speak.

  ▶ Common words are: more, please, thank you, eat, and milk

Keeping Your Home Safe When Baby Is on the Move

Babyproofing before your baby hits the next stage is crucial. You don't want to realize you need to put a gate at the stairs because your child suddenly figured out how to crawl when you ran to the bathroom for 30 seconds. When you're babyproofing, get down on the ground and crawl around for a bit. Yes, it may feel silly but doing so will help you figure out what risky situations your baby may get into. We know the basics like locking cabinets and drawers and putting baby gates on stairs or blocking outlets, but don't forget about hard surfaces like fireplace hearths or coffee table corners. Putting foam strips on the edges can prevent head injuries if your baby falls (they tend to have terrible balance). Be sure that anything they could grip to pull up on is secured to the wall and won't tip, and ensure carpets and rugs will not trip them or slip under them.

9–12 Months

The last part of the first year is bittersweet! Your child will be playing and exploring in all new manners. They will have emotions and maybe even strongly held opinions. By now your baby will probably be pulling up on furniture to get into a standing position and may have even taken their first few steps!

How you can help:

- Although you should use baby gates, teach your baby how to safely go up and down the stairs to prevent injuries from falls.

- Be sure to read to your baby daily.

- Start teaching your baby songs like "ABC Song" and "Twinkle, Twinkle, Little Star."

Tracking Your Baby's Health Is Helpful

Tracking your baby's health is important when there are concerns that need to be addressed. Timelines and diaries can provide crucial information for health care providers to investigate concerns. Furthermore, keeping track of things like sleeping and feeding is a great way for you to communicate your concerns with providers, especially if you switch providers at any point. That said, I caution you not to become too obsessed with record-keeping, especially if your child is healthy. Although analytic types love data, over-tracking basic nuances that come with the territory of having a baby can breed anxiety. Make sure you find a healthy balance!

Sleep, Feedings, and Diaper Changes Are a Great Place to Start

Whether or not to track feeds and diapers is up to you. If your baby was born full-term and healthy, it may not be necessary to keep detailed records of sleep, feeds, and diaper changes. If you've spoken with your health care provider and have concerns about health and weight gain, tracking can be very useful. So my advice to new parents is to keep a mental record of how often you're feeding and diapering the first few days, and if you're becoming concerned about anything, then start writing it down. When I see clients for lactation support, my first questions revolve around patterns in sleeping, eating, diapering, and weight gain/loss, so having this information can come in handy.

THERE ARE MANY HELPFUL TRACKERS ONLINE
There are a plethora of free apps and website programs that can assist you in keeping track of your baby's feeding and diapering. Or, you can easily make a daily chart on your computer or with old-fashioned pen and paper that lists the time you began and ended your feed, any notes about the feed, when you changed diapers, and any notes about the characteristics of the diapers.

Schedule Regular Checkups

Your health care provider will likely schedule a checkup on your baby two days after hospital discharge. After this, depending on your baby's health status, you may have frequent weight checks or bilirubin checks. Over the course of the first year, pediatricians will typically recommend periodic wellness checks to ensure your baby is meeting milestones and to discuss immunizations.

In addition to these wellness visits, I often recommend that parents seek care with a chiropractor or craniosacral therapist for their newborn. Craniosacral therapy (CST) helps ease tension around baby's mouth, head, and neck, as well as align the body. This may help with breastfeeding and getting the baby's system (eating, pooping, sleeping) working properly. Research shows CST can also help with colic. It is always important to take a multidisciplinary approach to wellness, and there is no better time to start than at the beginning of your baby's life.

What to Expect during a Growth Spurt

Growth spurts are a time when your baby will experience rapid development physically and mentally. They will begin to display new skills and a new level of understanding and communication skills. These big changes can also make babies cranky and uncomfortable, which is extra challenging for both baby and parents. So, what are some signs your baby is going through a growth spurt?

- Sleep patterns change
- More napping
- Increased fussiness
- Increased nursing/demand for feeding
- Clinginess

How to Cope with Growth Spurts

First, recognize a growth spurt for what it is and accept it. On a more practical level, you may need to reorganize your schedule. If you're mid–growth spurt, this may be a good time to minimize outings and focus on relaxing with your baby as much as possible. When you have things that must be done, babywearing, or "wearing" your baby in a wrap or carrier that allows you to be hands-free, can meet your baby's need for closeness and even increase appetite for breastfed babies (if you learn how to babywear and breast-feed simultaneously). Remember, if all the chores don't get done for a day or two, you can get back to them next week! Ask friends and family for help if you need it, too.

Regularly Check Your Baby's Nails, Ears, Eyes, Nose, and Mouth

Checking your baby's nails, eyes, ears, nose, and mouth will become second nature after a while. It can be surprising how much danger your little one can find themselves in with just their own hands! From scratching their faces with long nails to hiding food in their nose or cheeks, babies always keep things interesting.

While we're talking about fingers and toes: Make sure you keep an eye out for loose hairs that can wrap around baby appendages (toes, fingers, and even penises) creating a "hair tourniquet" that cuts off blood circulation.

Trimming Baby Nails

Most infant hygiene kits come with special baby nail clippers to help prevent hurting your baby when you trim their nails. During the early days, their nails are thin so you may be able to just file them down and avoid clippers. But as they grow, clippers will be more effective. I hate trimming baby nails, so what I've learned to do is clip nails while baby is sleeping in the car seat. If I don't get them all and baby wakes up, I get back to it during the next nap. I refuse to fight a baby's tight fists and flailing arms in the name of nail clipping.

Cleaning Out Noses, Eyes, and Ears

During bath time, make a habit of checking their ears for wax buildup. Although you should never stick anything deep into your baby's ear, remember to clean out the wax and dirt that has worked its way in. It's important to prevent buildup that could later impact hearing. Many newborns will be born with a clogged tear duct, so you may need to regularly wipe their eyes with a warm washcloth. As your baby grows and explores, regularly check their nose and mouth as babies love to hide little items or small food pieces in their nose or cheeks.

Teething Can Start Early

Did you know some babies are born with teeth? Yep! Natal teeth are a thing. That said, although most babies tend to get their first teeth around the middle of the first year, a pre-teething stage can start sooner than this. Your baby may begin gnawing on toys, their hands, or even your hands, and slobbering everywhere. This means that your baby is in the early stages of teething. There are many teething remedies, from gum oils to homeopathic pain relievers.

However, you should never apply numbing agents to your baby's gums. This can affect their ability to move their tongue, which can negatively impact feeding and, in rare cases, their airway. These products often include the active ingredient lidocaine, which the FDA warns could cause seizures or even heart failure if ingested by infants.

HOW TO CARE FOR YOUR BABY'S GUMS AND TEETH

Our dentist told us that once our baby starts eating food, we should wipe his gums with a washcloth at night to teach the habit of evening oral care. Once your baby begins developing teeth, you can continue the washcloth or introduce a soft bristled toothbrush. Keep oral care fun and relaxed in the first year.

Health Issues to Look Out For

During the first year, anytime your baby is unwell you may be tempted to run straight to the doctor. But it's also impractical to run to the doctor every time your baby is not feeling their best. It can be hard to figure out what is urgent, emergent, and what you can safely monitor at home.

As a former nurse, I tend to be more laid-back with sick kids and take a wait-and-see approach, using diagnostic and triage skills I learned over the years. However, it is important that you know you have resources available. Your insurance may have a nurse advice line and your pediatrician's office likely has a nurse triage line that you can contact if you're ever unsure of how to manage a health concern.

Fevers

Fevers are common in kids for a variety of reasons. Here are the rules of thumb for fever management:

- Fevers are the body's way of fighting an infection and do not always need to be subdued.

- A fever is a core temperature of 100.4°F.

- Fevers in newborns (two months and younger) are an emergency.

  ▶ Do not use a fever reducer without consulting a pediatrician first.

- Fevers in older infants can typically be self-managed.

  ▶ Lukewarm bath, skin to skin

  ▶ Fever reducers

  ▶ Acetaminophen is considered safe in babies as young as newborn. Be sure to consult your provider for dosing instructions.

  ▶ Ibuprofen is considered unsafe before six months. Be sure to consult your provider for dosing instructions.

Letting a fever run its course can be beneficial for ridding the body of the antigen. I tend to recommend fever reducers as a last resort, based on your child's behavior, not just temperature. A fever in a baby feeding well is different than a fever in a baby screaming in pain and refusing to feed. Although a fever can be normal, if it lasts longer than a day or two and is accompanied with other symptoms, it is crucial to consult with your health care provider. Be sure to keep track of any medications you provide and what time they were administered.

Rashes

Rashes can be totally benign, a sign of allergies, or a sign of a viral infection. Rashes are one of those things that are very common but still cause parents to panic. Not all rashes are the same. Rashes from allergens typically appear as raised bumps and redness whereas a viral rash may be more like large splotches over the skin. Be sure to take pictures before treating a rash. There are various topical treatments available over the counter for different rashes, but be sure to consult your health care provider before use. Important things to consider with a rash:

- Child's comfort level (does it seem itchy or is it unnoticed by your child?)
- Recent infections/viruses
- New medications or foods
- New clothing
- Use of new laundry detergents, soaps, etc.

Ear Infections

Ear infections are another common childhood ailment that can be very frustrating to deal with in the first year of life. Babies can't always communicate that they have ear pain and infections can go undiagnosed.

Signs and symptoms to watch for:

- Fever and unexplained pain or excessive screaming/crying

- Pulling on/touching ear

- Drainage from ear

- Difficulty balancing (mostly noticeable in walking children)

If you suspect that your child has an ear infection, contact your health care provider immediately to develop a care plan. Although there are home remedies that can be effective for ear infections, medical attention may be necessary. Frequent ear infections can require a procedure where semipermanent tubes are placed in your child's ears to assist with drainage.

Colds

Colds, also known as upper-respiratory infections, are common in young children. Although colds are necessary for developing the immune system, they can be scary! A stuffed-up baby is usually uncomfortable and cranky and there isn't much you can do to help. Thankfully, there are some home remedies that can make things a little better.

- Humidifiers can prevent dryness.

- Sitting in a steamy bathroom can loosen nasal secretions.

- Saline nasal spray: Look for gentle mists instead of harsh sprays (if you can, give things a test squirt).

- Nose aspirators, aka snot-suckers.

Anti-congestion medicines and vapor rubs can be dangerous for infants. Consult your provider before using any over-the-counter medications.

Managing Your Child's Vaccinations

Vaccination can be a very controversial topic for parents and doctors alike. Education is key in making the right decision for your family. The Centers for Disease Control and Prevention (CDC) has made information on vaccine ingredients, risks, and benefits available on their website. The CDC also has a Vaccine Adverse Event Reporting System (VAERS) that collects and analyzes data on adverse reactions with a goal of increasing vaccine safety. Be sure to discuss your questions, concerns, and religious beliefs regarding vaccination with your doctor.

Which Vaccines Are Recommended in Year One?

The CDC has published a universal vaccination schedule that is recommended for children. These vaccinations are typically offered at well-baby visits. Some parents with concerns about vaccinations may choose to space out vaccines in case there is a reaction so they can narrow down which vaccine is responsible.

Vaccines recommended in the first year include:

- Hepatitis B: 3 doses

- Rotavirus: 2 to 3 doses of oral vaccine

- DTaP (Covers Diphtheria, tetanus, and pertussis, also known as whooping cough): 3 doses

- HiB (Haemophilus influenzae type b): 2 to 3 doses

- PCV13 (Pneumococcal conjugate): 3 doses

- Inactivated poliovirus (IPV): 3 doses

- Influenza: annual 1 to 2 doses

- MMR (Measles, Mumps, Rubella): First dose at 12 months

- Varicella (chicken pox): First dose at 12 months

- Hepatitis A: First dose at 12 months

Conclusion

Being witness to the changes in growth and development over the first year of your child's life (and beyond) is a true gift. Even after having multiple children, I still welcome each heartwarming milestone with joy. Despite all the challenges that can come with parenting, witnessing the growth and changes and being a part of the smiles and fun is truly special.

REFLECTION PROMPT: *Baby books and growth apps can be a great way to keep track of your baby's development. Now is a great time to start looking for baby journals or playing with apps to find one you like to track your baby's growth and development.*

CHAPTER 8

Clothing, Toys, and Transportation

In this chapter we will learn about all the must-have baby items from clothes to toys, and my personal favorite baby gear: baby carriers. Make sure you read this chapter before you make your baby registry!

Baby Clothes Are So Cute, but What's Essential?

Tiny clothes are just so darn adorable. But what clothes will baby really need?

First of all, I don't recommend buying too many clothes before baby is born because you have no idea how big your baby will be at birth. My oldest was 8 lbs. 4 oz. at birth and wore newborn clothes for a few weeks. My second was 9 lbs. 4 oz. at birth and could fit in newborn clothes for only about a week. The younger two babies were both 10 lb. 4 oz. at birth and neither fit in newborn size clothes, ever. By eight weeks old, both were wearing 3-6-month-old clothes. My point is, babies are born all different sizes and grow so fast in the early days. There is no need for 18 outfits in each size. They will be wasted. Another thing to consider is if you cloth diaper, you'll likely have to size up a bit, too.

In my own experience, kids tend to fit in 6 to 9 month clothes for the longest (starting before 6 months and sometimes stretching past 9 months), so it may make sense to have more outfits in this size range. You're also likely to get lots of clothes from people, so it helps to hold off on buying a lot the first few weeks.

Onesies

I recommend a minimum of eight onesies in your baby's size depending on how frequently you want to do laundry and what season your baby was born. My summer babies lived in only short-sleeved onesies from about 3 weeks old to 12 weeks old. Winter babies may utilize onesies as a base layer under pants and a shirt, or a sleeper.

Sleepers

Again, depending on how frequently you do laundry, you may need only three to five sleepers on hand. I recommend avoiding sleepers with snaps (especially the ones where you have to snap together pant legs) and getting zipper sleepers instead. When buying nighttime clothes, think about the easiest way to clothe baby at 4 a.m. on two hours' sleep.

ROMPERS AND DRESSES

I'm of the opinion that little girls can never have too many rompers and dresses, but according to my husband, we really only need one for each day of the week—and two for Sunday. Responsible me recommends waiting until your baby is about three months old to overindulge on the cute outfits. That's when you'll probably be going out and about more.

What Should I Look For?

What do you value? Price points? Style? Sustainability? You can typically find some very cute clothes for low price points, but they may not be the most well-made clothing items. Organic cotton outfits seem to last the longest whereas thin synthetics seem to wear down easier and faster.

Consignment stores can also be a great option for buying quality clothes at a lower price. Some parents will consign clothes that were never or barely worn, and you can purchase them for a fraction of the retail cost. The best part is that sometimes you can trade in the clothes your baby has outgrown for a credit toward your purchase.

Safety First

The Consumer Product Safety Commission (CPSC) is a government organization tasked with creating safety guidelines for products. They have many guidelines for children's products. One requirement is that pajamas for infants younger than nine months must be flame-resistant. Another important rule they have for clothing manufacturers is that clothes do not contain choking hazards, meaning that decorative trims like lace cannot hang off the fabric more than a quarter-inch.

If you would like to avoid flame-retardant clothing, the CPSC recommends ensuring that the clothes are tight-fitting because this reduces fire hazards as well.

Easy On, Easy Off

Dressing babies isn't necessarily the easiest or most fun task in the world. This is why I recommend avoiding snaps and opting for zippers whenever possible. Diaper changes mean you need to remove layers of clothes and too many snaps and such will end up simply being a waste of your time and sanity.

When Will My Baby Start Playing with Toys?

Once your baby is alert, they will begin exploring their world. Babies as young as four to six weeks like to have something they can grasp in their hand. Hanging toys over a floor mat can be fun for even newborns to look at. At around three to four months old, they may even start batting at the toys. This is a good age to introduce crinkly fabric toys and textured silicone teethers. By six months old, your child will likely be making everything they find a toy. They will especially love toys that make shaking sounds or that they can roll. Toys that suction cup to the table can be a lifesaver when you go out to a restaurant or anywhere it may be hard to keep baby entertained.

Sometimes parents run out of play ideas and consider introducing baby shows at an early age. The American Academy of Pediatrics recommends that children under the age of

18 months not be exposed to screen time, except for video chats (because this is interactive). As an alternative, you could find interactive books to look at with your baby.

The Importance of Play

Play is the work of childhood. Your child's only job is literally to play in order to learn. When your child plays, they learn about physical properties: texture, weight, strength required to move something, taste, and so much more. But that's not all! Your child is also learning about cause and effect, how things fit together, and ultimately, how the world operates. What does the carpet taste like? What happens when you pull on a plant leaf hanging down? The lessons learned during playtime are literally setting a foundation for how the entire world operates. I'd say that's a pretty important lesson to learn!

Toys That Are Best for Every Stage in Year One

Truthfully, a bored kid will make a toy out of anything—which is pretty fantastic when you think about it. But what are the best toys for children during the first year?

0–6 MONTHS: Playmats with overhead hanging toys, rattles, teethers, fabric sensory books, and toys that encourage grip development. Avoid toys with small parts that could become a choking hazard.

6–12 MONTHS: Toys that encourage hand-eye coordination and gross motor skills are perfect! This can include stacking blocks, push toys, and more. Not sure how to decide? It can help to take your baby on playdates or to a local play café and see what toys they show an interest in.

Taking Baby on the Road

Traveling with baby is quite an undertaking. Whether it's a day trip to the zoo or a vacation across the country, you will be surprised how much stuff such a little person needs. From carriers to strollers, there is a whole world of baby travel gear to be explored. You're obviously going to want to consider budget and safety, but don't overlook convenience and lifestyle. City moms who take buses and trains have different needs than suburban moms who drive everywhere. So although online reviews are great, remember to talk to the moms in your area for insight on what's best for your situation.

Carriers

There are many kinds of carriers on the market and they come in varying quality. With baby carriers, you get what you pay for. So what are your options?

The most common options for frequent babywearing are a ring sling, wrap, or soft-structured carrier. Ring slings are a long fabric that utilizes belt loop–like rings to adjust tension on the fabric to secure your baby against your body. Although it looks hard to do at first, you'll quickly get the hang of it with some practice. Wraps are even longer strips of fabric that are woven to be strong enough to support the weight of your baby. This fabric is wrapped around you and your baby to secure them against your body. This also takes a lot of practice to learn, but many people love this option.

Soft-structured carriers typically have straps that clip together to make babywearing quick and secure. These carriers tend to be sturdier than wraps and slings, though they may also seem bulkier.

Car Seats

Car seats for kiddos in their first year come in two forms: infant carriers and convertible car seats. Both are suitable for newborns, and which one you choose really comes down to preference.

There are some important universal rules for car seat safety:

- Infants must be rear-facing during the first two years, and should remain that way until they max out their weight limit on the seat or turn four years old.

- It is crucial to ensure that your child's chest clip is at the right location and the straps fit properly.

- Do not ever dress baby in a puffy coat or thick layers of clothing under the car seat straps. Instead, dress baby warm and use blankets over the straps to keep baby cozy.

A good car seat can last you a few years, so think about cleaning and maintenance as you make your decision, too. Also, if you're unsure how to install your car seat, there are many tutorial videos online. You can also check in with your local fire department or police station because they often have certified staff members who can check your car for you.

Strollers

There are many kinds of strollers on the market. When choosing a stroller you should consider whether you need one that accommodates an infant seat or not. Additionally, you should consider how much space it will take up in your trunk, the kind of wheels it has, and the activities you'll be using it for.

Taking Your Baby on an Airplane

In the United States, an infant younger than two years old is permitted to fly as a "lap child," which means that the child does not need a ticket and will sit on parents' laps during the flight. However, for safety purposes it is recommended that a child sit in their own seat, and parents bring their car seat on the plane. This can protect your child during hard landings. Pacifiers, breastfeeding, and lollipops can help their ears pop as they change altitudes; otherwise, they may cry at the new, uncomfortable sensation.

Getting Comfortable Leaving Your Baby with Others

Everyone has a different philosophy on leaving their child with other caretakers. It is usually pretty difficult for a new mom to spend time away from her baby, especially if she is still trying to establish breastfeeding. However, leaving your baby with others will usually become a reality at some point during the first year. Finding a caretaker you trust is key. You may need to just do short outings to start off and gradually increase to longer outings. For instance, you could leave your baby with your partner while you take a 20-minute walk around the neighborhood. Once you're comfortable with this you can upgrade to going out to treat yourself to a meal, time at the library, or whatever else you enjoy for an hour. Eventually, you will find what your and your baby's limits are for separation.

Tips for Dealing with Separation Anxiety

Separation anxiety is a reality for both parents and baby when experiencing separations.

For the parents: You've done your due diligence vetting your caregiver. It's okay to spend a little bit of time away from your baby. To help you feel more comfortable, one option is using a surveillance camera that can feed straight to your smartphone so you can always check in.

For baby: Getting your baby familiar with their caregiver can make separation anxiety smoother but doesn't always eliminate it. Sometimes it helps for baby to keep a favorite toy close or have a blanket nearby that smells like Mom or Dad. Start with small separations so your baby can learn that you always return, and gradually increase separation as your baby copes better.

Navigating Childcare

Finding trusted childcare can be challenging, especially because your baby can't talk to tell you if they feel safe with their new caretaker. But this isn't just stressful for baby—it's difficult for you, too. You need to communicate feeding plans, nap schedules, and other nuances in your child's care that have become second nature to you. I highly recommend running a background check on a potential babysitter, then inviting them to come spend a day with you and your baby, getting to know your family and your needs. This will allow you to see how the caregiver interacts with your child and if they are a good fit for your family. You can have the caregiver focus on baby while you get some household tasks taken care of or just go take a shower! This way your little one can get used to alone time with the new person, but you aren't far away. By the time your new sitter flies solo, your little one will see them as a familiar face and not a new stranger. Whether you're utilizing a childcare service, a family member, or a local teenager during date night, one thing remains the same: Open and clear communication of expectations is vital.

You and Your Baby Will Have So Much Fun Together

After you escape the newborn fog and begin playing and exploring the world with your baby, life becomes fun again. It may be a different kind of fun than what you were used to pre-baby, but this family kind of fun is so special in its own way. Watching your little one experience the world and learn new things will bring you a unique type of joy that you didn't know before parenthood. Don't be afraid to get out there and make those memories with your little one. Remember, even if your baby doesn't actually remember details from that zoo trip when they were five months old, they are still laying down synapses in their brain and learning so much about the world. Make the most of it!

Enjoy the Ride

Getting out with baby can be challenging, but it's worth it. You will laugh and you will cry and you will get frustrated. It's part of being a parent. The best part of this is that your baby isn't the only one learning. You'll be continually learning new things about yourself as you watch your baby learn and grow. Enjoy this ride. Don't take it for granted.

Conclusion

So, do we agree that playing and exploring the world are super important for your baby? The first year is so full of many transitions and changes for both you and your baby. Just remember that you are a family now and your baby is not against you. Learning how to embrace your baby's need to play in order to grow and how to balance your own self-care with that is no easy feat, but it is doable.

REFLECTION PROMPT: *Discuss with your significant other how much you intend to travel and explore with your baby. Use these plans to figure out what some special "must-have" baby items may be. Also, start talking about what your plans will be for childcare during work or date nights, and how you can make this experience easier for you and your baby. In the next section, we will dive deeper into baby's growth and development by age.*

PART THREE

Keeping Track of Your Baby's Growth and New Parent FAQs

It is important to remember that all new parents worry. It's even more important to remember that our reasons for worrying are usually rooted in lack of experience, lack of knowledge, or just plain fear. Hopefully, the first two parts of this book armed you with enough knowledge to conquer some of those fears. Which is good, because this section of the book will deal with one of the scariest things of all: baby milestones. It gives details on each milestone and includes commonly asked questions new parents will have. It should help ease your concerns as you welcome your baby into your new life together.

CHAPTER 9

Your Baby Month by Month

When planning what I would cover in this book, I reached out to social media, as any modern-day mom would do, and asked all the parents out there what their top questions were as new parents. Everyone said, "Milestones!" One especially brand-new mama shared that she was eagerly awaiting the next pediatrician appointment to ask if she should be looking for any specific milestones in her one-month-old because she's constantly worried if he's ahead or behind. At one month! So if you're feeling anxious about your baby's milestones, remember that you're not alone. But you're likely worrying over nothing. It is really important to remember that milestone markers are simply guidelines and babies are rarely "behind" or "advanced"; they're just on their own path. Your health care provider will be able to offer a full assessment of your baby's growth and development to let you know if there is reason for worry. Try to frame these milestones as things to "look forward to" instead of things to "watch out for." Your baby is full of surprises and milestone lists are meant to help you prepare for some of them, not stress out if they miss a couple.

Month 1

Growth—During the first month of your baby's life, so many changes occur. They go from a squished-up raisin to looking like a baby doll. You may notice that baby's skin has changed. It may be splotchy, dry or peeling, or have baby acne. Gentle lotions can be helpful, but there's nothing you usually need to do for any of these conditions. By two weeks old, you should expect your baby to be back to birth weight and gaining 5 to 8 ounces per week.

Sleeping—Expect your newborn to be sleeping more often than not! We discussed earlier that newborns sleep a lot; they just do it in short bursts. So, I said it before, and I'll say it again: Sleep when baby sleeps!

Eating—It will seem like your baby wants to eat constantly. Remember that they are used to a constant supply of nutrition and never felt hunger before. Now that they're earthside, hunger will dominate their life and yours. About 12 feeds a day is within normal range.

Bowel Movements—After the first week of life, don't be surprised if your baby poops every time they feed. Although there can be a wide range of normal, if your one-month-old goes longer than 24 hours without pooping, call your pediatrician.

Watch for It—My absolute favorite with newborns is that they will smile in their sleep. Before the end of the first month, your baby is likely to start making eye contact with you purposefully and it can bring a whole new feeling of falling in love!

Key Developments

MENTAL/EMOTIONAL—Your baby is still very sleepy but each day you'll notice that they grow more alert and aware of their surroundings.

PHYSICAL—Your baby is still very reflex-centered and will bring fists to mouth or start rooting as early feeding cues.

SENSORY—Newborns can't see very far. In fact, they can only see about 8 to 10 inches in front of them. Interestingly enough, this is about the same distance from the breast to Mom's face! How sweet is that?!

VERBAL—Most communication skills come in the form of crying. But soon they will start learning new ways of communicating with you. In the meantime, talk to them as much as you can. It helps.

SOCIAL—Your baby's love language is snuggles and feeding. Your newborn probably won't want to interact much with someone who isn't providing one of those two necessities.

Bonding with a Baby—Skin to skin! I don't care if you breast-feed, bottle-feed, or your baby has a nasogastric tube (which is used for feeding medically complex babies). Skin to skin is crucial for your baby's development and can aid in bonding. Both baby and parent should be topless, snuggled up with skin in direct contact, and a light blanket laid over them to keep the heat in. Not only is skin-to-skin contact crucial for regulating baby's breathing, heart rate, and temperature, but also it evokes hormonal responses from parents that support bonding.

Baby Care Tip—Keep a mental note or physical log of how often your baby feeds, pees, and poops each day to assess whether they are getting enough to eat.

Self-Care Tip—Sleep when baby sleeps! You'll need lots of sleep and help during the first month. Ask your friends and family for help with prepping meals or providing a meal train. And don't be afraid of ordering takeout when you need it, too.

Month 2

Growth—In the second month you can expect your baby to grow at about one inch per month and gain about one to two pounds, and look a little squishier!

Sleeping—Your baby is likely still sleeping about 15 hours per day, but may have started a more predictable sleeping pattern.

Eating—Babies should still be fed on demand. Babies being bottle-fed breast milk should receive about 3 to 4 ounces per feed every two to four hours. Formula-fed babies will typically drink around 4 to 5 ounces per bottle at this age.

Bowel Movements—Expect at least three bowel movements per day though there is a wide range of normal. It can be common for breastfed babies older than six weeks to go up to seven days without having a bowel movement. Although daily stooling is ideal, most health care providers are not concerned with older breastfed babies skipping a few days between poops.

Key Developments

MENTAL/EMOTIONAL—Your baby will recognize familiar sights and sounds, so sing songs and talk to your baby throughout the day to stimulate their development. Toys that hang above them on a playmat or swing can be very entertaining for them at this age as their eyesight develops.

PHYSICAL—Some babies may be enjoying tummy time, developing head control, and even rolling over or scooting. Your baby may also be developing coordination skills, now capable of purposely bringing their hand to their mouth.

SENSORY—Your baby will start to recognize objects and the faces of loved family members.

VERBAL—Two-month-old babies start to coo and make more purposeful noises. They may also turn toward sounds they hear. So make sure you practice imitating their sounds and making your own for them to learn.

SOCIAL—During the second month of life, if they haven't already, your baby will start smiling socially in response to parents and family interactions.

Watch for It—Remember that hand-eye coordination that is starting to develop? If your baby uses pacifiers you may just notice that during the second month your baby is able to push the pacifier back in their mouth when it falls out (if it's still close by).

Bonding with a Baby—Take a walk while babywearing and describe the items you pass. Stand close to a tree, for example, and allow your baby to look at the details. You can also start introducing them to picture books for visual stimulation.

Baby Care Tip—Say the names of objects and items your baby is examining to help them learn about the world around them. Be descriptive! This helps them learn concepts like colors, numbers, and shapes, too.

Self-Care Tip—If you're the birth parent you may have been recently cleared for activity and exercise by your doctor. Getting exercise is a great way to help prevent the effects of postpartum depression, so start introducing walks and see if you may be up for some Pilates or other gentle exercising.

Month 3

Growth—Your baby has probably sized out of diapers a few times now and maybe even a few outfits, too. You'll notice your baby is getting nice and chubby. Their hair may start falling out and growing back in a different texture or color during this month.

Sleeping—Although your baby still sleeps quite a bit, wake times are longer and more entertaining. Your baby is likely to experience a growth spurt and overnight sleep patterns may change temporarily.

Eating—Your baby may go longer between demanding feeds and may be more distracted during feeding.

Bowel Movements—Stool will remain the yellowish seedy consistency you have grown accustomed to.

Key Developments

MENTAL/EMOTIONAL—Your baby will insist on not just being fed and diapered, but also included in your daily activities. This is a sign they're observing more of their world and are eager to explore.

PHYSICAL—Your baby is likely rolling and scooting and may even pull up into a sitting position when grasping your fingers.

SENSORY—Your baby's hearing and vision begins developing more rapidly. They will look closely and begin studying things, and this includes using their mouth!

VERBAL—Your three-month-old is much more verbal. Coos sound more intentional and seem to express emotions like joy and curiosity. Keep talking and matching sounds.

SOCIAL—Your baby is starting to become really fun to engage and interact with and will begin to recognize familiar faces.

Watch for It—Three-month-olds love to pull on hair and jewelry, so watch out! This is also when a lot of moms will go to the salon for a "mom cut" and get their hair shorter so it's more challenging for baby to pull. My personal preference, however, is the perpetual messy bun.

Bonding with a Baby—My favorite way to play with three-month-olds is by making funny faces and silly sounds. They're fun! They're also a fun way to engage with baby.

Baby Care Tip—As your baby starts grasping everything and doing more exploring, keep an eye out for stray hairs that may have wrapped tightly around their fingers (and toes, even). These can cut off circulation and cause a lot of discomfort or injury.

Self-Care Tip—You've made it through the "fourth trimester" and deserve to celebrate! If your baby is giving you a little bit of a break (i.e., sleeping longer between feeds) you may be feeling a little more energized, so take this opportunity to do something for you. Think about all the things you've put off the last three months and pick something that will bring you joy. You've earned it!

Month 4

Growth—Your baby's weight gain will likely slow down to around 3.5 to 4.5 ounces per week. Babies grow in spurts so don't panic if they plateau for a few weeks because they can catch up all at once.

Sleeping—Sleep is a roller coaster. As you head into the fourth month, you can expect some sleep disturbances thanks to developmental changes. Your baby's brain does a lot of work at night so try to remind yourself that those sleepless nights have a valuable purpose.

Eating—Just when you thought you were getting the hang of things, your baby may start crying a lot while eating. This probably doesn't indicate anything other than that your baby is having a hard time focusing on eating with so many interesting distractions around! It can be helpful to establish a consistent feeding routine to help them focus and feel comfortable.

Bowel Movements—Stool remains unchanged until you introduce food.

Key Developments

MENTAL/EMOTIONAL—The "four-month fussies" (as La Leche League calls it) are in full swing. Your baby is taking in everything and it can be a lot to process! Just keep in mind this is developmentally normal and not necessarily an indication that anything is "wrong."

PHYSICAL—Your baby's coordination and strength are improving a lot this month! Look for your baby to improve their scooting and rolling skills. They won't look so shocked every time they roll over. They also may start pushing up on their arms during tummy time!

SENSORY—Your baby will study everything from patterns to your own actions and behaviors. You may even catch your little one growing interested in the television if you have it on. Be conscious of this because the American Academy of Pediatrics advises limited to no screen time for children younger than two years old.

VERBAL—Your baby's coos are more robust and your baby may sound like they're trying to have a conversation with you, cooing in response to your words.

SOCIAL—Your baby will be developing clear relationships with familiar family members and caregivers. This is the age when my own kiddos started to connect with their siblings and lean toward Daddy for playtime when they were done with feedings.

Watch for It—Your baby is pretty active! Tummy time is really fun now because your baby will scoot around with a goal in mind. Put some toys just out of reach to encourage that army crawl.

Bonding with a Baby—Your baby will enjoy smiling at your silly faces, listening to music, and playing games with toys. My kids always love mirror play at this age. We make funny faces in the mirror and they love to react to the reflections.

Baby Care Tip—Your baby may need a dark, quiet place to feed if they're having a hard time settling down and focusing on feeding. Feeding your baby while babywearing can sometimes help, especially if your baby will tolerate a cover to block out distractions.

Self-Care Tip—A fussy baby can be very overwhelming even if you know it's developmentally appropriate. You may be struggling with getting ready to go back to work or you may just be feeling tired of being the primary caretaker for your child during this month. It's okay to feel like everything is *not* okay. Lean on your support system. Talk about how you're feeling and see if someone can give you a break somehow, depending on what you need.

Month 5

Growth—Your baby has probably doubled their birth weight by now! If not, they'll be very close to double, which also means that you may be feeling sore from carrying that chunk around!

Sleeping—Sometimes around five months, you get a little break between growth spurts and your baby's sleeping patterns may feel sustainable for once.

Eating—If your baby is formula-fed, you're likely feeding closer to 6 to 8 ounces per feed by now. Make sure you're still pacing feeds and consulting your health care provider for how many total ounces your baby needs. Because formula takes longer to digest, your baby may go longer between feeds than their breast-fed counterparts (this is not a hard-and-fast rule, though).

Bowel Movements—There's not much change here yet.

Key Developments

MENTAL/EMOTIONAL—Your baby is learning cause and effect at this age. This is why you may feel like they are making a very annoying game out of dropping their toy and having you pick it up. I promise, they're not trying to be frustrating; they're laughing about it because they think it's cool to learn this concept!

PHYSICAL—Your five month-old may be sitting up unassisted for short periods of time. You can use a Boppy pillow to help support them as they develop strength to sit.

SENSORY—Your baby is seeing the full rainbow now, although they will likely prefer primary colors. They are also able to see without crossing their eyes. But they still don't have 20/20 vision just yet.

VERBAL—Your baby will start making "ma-ma" or "da-da" sounds but likely has not yet attached meaning to the sounds. But don't worry, your baby will be intentionally calling for you soon!

SOCIAL—Your five-month-old is likely to respond to affection with a smile, and smile at others intentionally to get a reaction.

Watch for It—Your baby may start trying to grab food off your plate and show a major interest in eating. A little taste probably won't hurt but know that the World Health Organization and CDC both recommend waiting until six months to offer your baby solid foods.

Bonding with a Baby—Because your baby is more alert and aware of the world around them, this may be a fun age to start taking your baby to a zoo or aquarium for a change of scenery.

Baby Care Tip—Double-check your babyproofing! Make sure wires and other dangerous items are put away safely. Your baby is putting everything in their mouth and if they're scooting and rolling, this can put them in dangerous situations.

Self-Care Tip—Check in with yourself and your partner or trusted caregiver this month. Set aside some quiet time to talk about what you've learned about yourself and each other. Remember that parenting is an opportunity to grow. Allowing yourself this time to connect with yourself and your support team can help you avoid getting overwhelmed.

Month 6

Growth—You love your baby's gummy grin, but get ready. Your baby is likely to start sporting a one-tooth jack-o'-lantern smile any day now!

Sleeping—Your baby's sleep habits may be just getting predictable and then suddenly change thanks to teething and more brain development.

Eating—Although breast milk or formula should still be the main source of your baby's nutrition, it is now recommended to start introducing solid foods if your baby meets the milestones. (Check the baby-led weaning section on page 52.)

Bowel Movements—Introducing foods may make your baby's poop more solid and stinky. Ensure that your baby is receiving enough breast milk/formula to prevent constipation as you introduce solids, too.

Key Developments

MENTAL/EMOTIONAL—Babies this age are typically content and happy. They will use sounds to express emotions as joyful and even sad or frustrated.

PHYSICAL—Your baby is becoming a pro with the palmar grasp and fine-tuning the pincer grasp. Your baby has likely lost the tongue thrust reflex and is sitting unassisted. Teeth may start popping through.

SENSORY—Your baby is learning about the whole world with every sense of their body. Feeding times are especially good exercises for sensory play! Let them squish, taste, and smell foods.

VERBAL—Your baby's coos may be turning into words like mama or dada; if not, they will at least sound more intentional and conversational. If you're interested in teaching baby sign language, this is a great time to start.

SOCIAL—Your baby probably responds to their own name by now and seems to communicate much more intentionally.

Watch for It—Your baby may start pushing up to all fours, rocking back and forth, and possibly even crawling. Keep that phone handy to record these precious memories.

Bonding with a Baby—Babies this age are starting to play in more advanced ways. Your baby may enjoy playing with stacking blocks or cups. Although they likely won't start stacking them purposely until closer to a year, they will begin banging the blocks together and learning how to use them.

Baby Care Tip—If your baby is sitting unassisted, bath time can move from the baby bath to the "big bath." Peek-a-boo starts to become a more entertaining game for your baby as they gain more object permanence.

Self-Care Tip—You may be feeling a little worn out at this stage, especially if your baby is experiencing a growth spurt and struggling to sleep. Something I loved to do when my babies were around this age was to put them in the car for nap time and go for a ride to my favorite drive-thru. My baby would get a nap, and I would get some much-needed quiet time outside the house. If you don't have a car, try working a stroller nap into the routine and walk to get a treat or bring a snack from home to a quiet spot nearby.

Month 7

Growth—Around seven months old, your baby starts looking more like a big kid! They will be longer and heavier and have much more coordination with each passing day.

Sleeping—Sleep may continue to be inconsistent this month, alternating between solid sleep and disturbances related to growth spurts and teething.

Eating—If you're practicing baby-led weaning, you may find that your baby is starting to actually get food in their mouth more than just smashing it. Experiment with some homemade baby foods to introduce new textures and flavors.

Bowel Movements—As your child continues to eat a more diverse diet, stools will likely be harder, darker, and more solid. Poop may change color based on different things your baby consumes. Ensure that they remain hydrated to avoid constipation.

Key Developments

MENTAL/EMOTIONAL—Sometime between four months and seven months, your baby will develop an understanding of object permanence.

PHYSICAL—Around seven months old, your little one should be bearing weight on their legs with support. Some overachievers may even be pulling themselves into standing positions using furniture or crib rails.

SENSORY—By now your baby's vision is much more robust. They will begin to develop their sense of depth perception as they explore their growing world.

VERBAL—Your baby may not be saying full words yet, but they may already be a babbling brook! Even though you don't understand your little bear's language, having conversations can help develop language skills.

SOCIAL—Babies this age really enjoy social play! If they have older siblings, they're very eager to be included in playtime. If not, setting up playdates is a fun way to introduce them to other kids.

Watch for It!—If your baby has started pulling up and you haven't already lowered the crib level, now is the time to do it. Don't wait for your baby to fall over the crib rail!

Bonding with a Baby—Because your baby is weight-bearing, it can be fun to introduce them to a toy like Jolly Jumper and put some music on to "dance" with them.

Baby Care Tip—Make sure that any furniture your baby can pull up on is anchored to the wall to prevent tipping.

Self-Care Tip—Your busy little one is likely to start taking a toll on your energy in a different way than the newborn phase. If you don't already have a daily routine set, now is the time to create one. Prioritize a few tasks that must get done in the morning and do them every morning. Likewise, prioritize a few tasks in the evening that must get done before you go to bed (to make the next day easier). In my house, the dishwasher must be loaded and turned on at night before bed, and it must be unloaded as early in the morning as possible. This allows us to stay on top of dishes and greatly reduces personal stress while eliminating the opportunity for an argument.

Month 8

Growth—By now, weight gain has likely slowed significantly to an average of 8 ounces per month.

Sleeping—Babies this age sleep around 14 hours total, usually including a morning nap and afternoon nap. A lot of parents will have tried at least one approach to sleep training by eight months old. You may be feeling hopeless at the never-ending roller coaster of great sleep and regular wake-ups. Remember what we talked about in chapter 5. Babies are primal creatures, even at eight months old, and sleep patterns aren't always linear.

Eating—Your baby is likely becoming more proficient with self-feeding by now. Your little one may even be able to feed themself with pre-loaded spoons.

Bowel Movements—The more table food your baby eats, the grosser the poop . . . but hey! It's a sign of good health in a lot of ways. Some food allergies may present as dramatic changes in bowel movements. Contact your pediatrician with any concerns.

Key Developments

MENTAL/EMOTIONAL—Around eight months old (give or take) your little one may develop separation anxiety or stranger danger.

PHYSICAL—Your baby is likely already crawling or about to start. Make sure you keep baby gates on your stairs now to be extra safe. Your baby will also have practiced enough grasping skills that they can start to play with some basic toys, too.

VERBAL—Your baby is likely mimicking your own sounds and inflection more frequently. They'll also begin understanding familiar words like "milk" or "bottle."

SOCIAL—Babies this age may start to wave "bye-bye" or "hello" and get noticeably excited to see familiar people. Encourage them!

Watch for It—Your little one may really start developing a sense of rhythm at this stage. They may even learn how to clap with you! Resist the urge to unleash your discography on them and start with simple nursery rhymes and sing-alongs.

Bonding with a Baby—If your baby is on the go, there may be fun local baby-gym classes to start attending with your little one.

Baby Care Tip—If your baby is spending a lot of time on the floor exploring, make sure to check the area for small items that could be choking hazards. Minimize risk of having hazards and germs tracked into the house by asking friends and family to remove their shoes at the door.

Self-Care Tip—Many breastfeeding women experience the return of their cycle during the second half of the first year. This can bring more hormonal shifts that can make you feel unsettled. The return of your cycle can also make breastfeeding temporarily challenging (such as sore nipples or slowed milk ejection reflex). Being aware of these potential changes can help you meet them with grace instead of anxiety. You can also prepare by ensuring that you are supporting your body with vital nutrients like iron, calcium, and magnesium.

Month 9

Growth—That jack-o'-lantern smile has probably progressed to something close to a full set of teeth . . . okay maybe not full, but that gummy grin is no more. You've got a full-grown child smiling up at you (so it may seem).

Sleeping—Your nine-month-old may start giving you some full nights of sleep, if they haven't already. However, every baby is different. If anyone tells you your baby doesn't need to wake up for a feeding at this age, just remember that you are the expert on your baby and it is okay to respond to your baby's needs.

Eating—Your baby should still be primarily fed breast milk or formula; however, they may be starting to eat more solid foods during meal times. Although food is still mainly for fun, your baby is probably fully enjoying snacks throughout the day and maybe even looking forward to them.

Bowel Movements—With all that food comes the risk of stopped-up bowels. Make sure you're offering a couple ounces of water throughout the day to reduce constipation.

Key Developments

MENTAL/EMOTIONAL—As their understanding of their world grows, your little one may get clingy and show clear preferences for favorite toys and people.

PHYSICAL—Lots of crawling now and baby may even be standing with help or on their own.

SENSORY—If you haven't already, start introducing your baby to sensory play such as crawling on different surfaces, playing with Jell-O, and more!

VERBAL—Your little one understands a lot more than they say. Particularly they understand the word "no" and may have no problem showing contempt in response. Your baby is probably saying "Mama" or "Dada" by now, and may even have a few other words up their sleeve. If not, just be patient and remember that all babies are different. Resist the urge to compare your child to a chatterbox their age.

Watch for It—Some early walkers may take their first steps around this age, so keep an eye out if your little one is particularly active.

Baby Care Tip—Bath time is especially fun, but may be dangerous with a baby who is pulling up and trying to stand and walk. Consider adding anti-slip stickers or mats to the tub.

Self-Care Tip—Even though you're not newly postpartum, postpartum depression can set in anytime during the first year, especially as hormones shift and change or life becomes more demanding. Familiarize yourself with the warning signs of depression and contact your health care provider immediately if you have any thoughts of harming yourself or your baby. Sometimes those thoughts happen, and it doesn't make you a bad parent; it's just a flag that you need to reach out for support.

Month 10

Growth—Your baby's weekly growth is still on the slower side, around 2 ounces per week. In fact, once your baby is on the go, it's not uncommon to see a minor and temporary weight loss (just a couple ounces). Discuss your baby's growth chart with your pediatrician if you have any concerns.

Sleeping—Your little one probably has a pretty great sleep routine down by now. An hour nap in the morning, an hour nap in the afternoon, and a solid stretch of overnight sleep!

Eating—Kiddos at this age can be really excited about solids. Parents need to be very careful to make sure they are offering breast milk or formula before and after every meal, ensuring that it is still the primary source of nutrition.

Bowel Movements—Stools are still harder, darker, and more solid. As your baby tries different food, you may notice that the poop changes colors. Continue monitoring hydration to avoid constipation.

Key Developments

MENTAL/EMOTIONAL—Your little one may seem to hit a major turning point at around 10 months old and suddenly seem not so baby-like anymore. They will develop preferences for certain tastes and textures and start to display curiosity about how items around them work.

PHYSICAL—By 10 months old your little bear is likely crawling, standing, and possibly even walking and climbing.

SENSORY—Your little one is truly on the go, experiencing the world with all five senses! The stimulation seems endless, which means they can sometimes get overstimulated. Remember to gradually decrease stimuli like lights and sounds as needed to make feeding and sleeping easier.

VERBAL—Your baby may begin to point at things while trying to say the name of the object. Jump in and help! Babies at this stage like to mimic people so don't be surprised if they start imitating you. They are also understanding more words than they can speak now, so they may understand simple commands.

SOCIAL—If you've taught your baby sign language, they're probably improving these skills and communicating well with basic signs.

Watch for It—Listen closely! Your baby is likely to say a new word you weren't ready for. And they may not say it again for a while. When my oldest was this age he yelled the dog's name, "Daisy!" clear as day when she was barking and then didn't say it again for three months.

Bonding with a Baby—Parks start being really fun with little ones as they become more mobile. Sliding and bouncing are fun times for babies. They also begin to really enjoy swings at this age.

Baby Care Tip—Even though your little one is probably walking, you don't need to put shoes on your baby. Going barefoot is ideal for supporting proper foot development. Firm, formed shoes can encourage poor development. Although being barefoot outside is totally okay, if you're uncomfortable with that or live in an environment where that is not an option, soft-soled moccasins can be a great middle ground.

Self-Care Tip—Have you found that ever since giving birth things don't seem quite right when you laugh and sneeze? A lot of biological mothers will find themselves leaking urine or experiencing painful sex after having a baby. Many times we think it will take care of itself, but months later we experience no improvement. If you haven't already, seek out a physical therapist who specializes in pelvic floor therapy. If you're struggling, they can be key to helping you get back some much-needed quality of life.

Month 11

Growth—Your baby's growth probably seems to have hit a "plateau" at this point or slowed dramatically. That's normal. Keep an eye on your baby's growth charts and discuss any concerns with your pediatrician.

Sleeping—Your baby may decide they no longer need a morning nap, and transition to one nap a day. As your little one drops their first nap, you may experience increased crankiness (from both of you) as your routines adjust.

Eating—Favorite foods at this age may include yogurt, fruit, cheese, crackers, scrambled eggs, and meats. For snacking on the go, you may like to utilize the squeeze pouches of pureed fruit or yogurt.

Bowel Movements—Your baby has more solid poops as they try different solid foods. Similar to previous months, continue to monitor dehydration and constipation.

Key Developments

MENTAL/EMOTIONAL—Your baby's personality traits are starting to shine through! Your baby is no longer a helpless little infant, but seems to be quickly turning into a toddler.

PHYSICAL—Your 11-month-old's coordination and balance are likely greatly improving. They can climb the stairs or maybe even walk with proficiency and without falling as much.

SENSORY—As your baby continues developing, you'll find that they enjoy making music or noise and love to discover new sounds. This is a good time to use softer, sleepy-time music to help baby wind down and decrease stimuli.

VERBAL—Your baby is imitating words and sounds more proficiently these days, and is more deeply understanding the meanings attached to words.

SOCIAL—Your baby loves to wave hello and goodbye.

Watch for It—Your baby loves imitating sounds so much at this age. They don't just imitate human sounds, they'll also start imitating your pets. You may catch your little one meowing like a kitten or barking like a puppy before they learn the word *cat* or *dog*.

Bonding with a Baby—Include your baby in household tasks and chores. If your baby is standing or walking, they will love to be given a rag to "clean" with. They can also help hand you silverware from the dishwasher or help push laundry from the dryer into the laundry basket.

Baby Care Tip—Your baby may find feeding time more fun than productive. If your little one doesn't finish a meal, that's okay! Just keep offering and introducing foods.

Self-Care Tip—Now that you're almost a year out from welcoming your baby and likely settled into a pretty solid routine, you may be thinking more about your own fitness and wellness goals. If you haven't already leveled up your postpartum fitness plan, now is a great time to start incorporating more intense workouts. Make sure you consult with your health care provider and a fitness trainer who specializes in postpartum fitness to help you reach your goals.

Month 12

Growth—Your baby is probably around 2.5 to 3 times their birth weight by one year old!

Sleeping—If you haven't already, you may be considering introducing baby to their own room or maybe even a toddler bed (depending on if they started figuring out how to climb out of the crib yet). Changes in sleep locations can cause a temporary disturbance in established sleep patterns. If you're weaning, that could also affect sleep. Be sure to gauge your baby's individual needs and your own and find an approach that works for you.

Eating—At 12 months, a lot of parents are thinking about weaning from the breast or the bottle. Breast milk and formula no longer need to be the primary source of nutrition, although the World Health Organization does recommend breastfeeding during the second year of life as well. In my experience as a lactation consultant and a mom, breastfed one-year-olds will sometimes act like newborns—feeding often, acting like they don't know how to latch, and being clingy and needy. This is likely a combination of mental development and seeking comfort for molars coming in.

Bowel Movements—As you start decreasing the amount of breast milk or formula your baby is eating and increasing table foods, you can expect some serious changes in poop and poop patterns. A healthy baby should still stool daily and not struggle with constipation.

Key Developments

MENTAL/EMOTIONAL—Your baby will suddenly seem like a toddler overnight. They have opinions and plans and may even act like the captain of the ship now!

PHYSICAL—Going to the park with your baby is going to be really fun now! Not only will they enjoy the swings, but also their increased balance and coordination skills mean they will love to climb and even try to run with the big kids. Finding a park with a baby-size jungle-gym will help keep your little one safe from big falls.

SENSORY—Because your baby is experiencing life in such a sensory way, now is a great time to introduce textured books and other interactive sensory learning.

VERBAL—Your baby may start saying two-syllable words or even putting two words together to make little sentences, but if your baby is still pretty quiet don't be alarmed. Just keep talking and reading to them and ask your pediatrician about variations for one-year-old speech development.

SOCIAL—Stranger danger is still a thing, but your little one may be learning how to feel safe around new people. They'll also start smiling and laughing more than ever.

Watch for It—Your little one is going to want to do everything the "big kids" do but probably has half the skill and no fear. Be ready for skinned knees and bumped noses.

Bonding with a Baby—Your baby is more of a toddler now so take them to social events if you haven't started to already. Library story times, local park meet-ups, and so much more can be a lot of fun! Finding mommy-and-me activities to participate in with your little bear will be a great opportunity not just for learning, but also for bonding with your baby.

Baby Care Tip—Your baby's first-birthday celebration is something worth looking forward to! Your little one will probably be ready to party but may get overtired very quickly. One-year-olds tend to be little balls of energy and then crash hard, so try to stick to your routines.

Self-Care Tip—You made it! One year! My tip to you is to celebrate your baby, then schedule a trusted sitter and go out to celebrate being a parent for one whole year! Make sure to include your partner or a reliable friend or family member who was there for you this year. If you've been sucked into and bogged down by parenting, use this opportunity to get to know each other better. You've likely both grown a lot over the last year as well!

CHAPTER 10

New Parent FAQs

Q. I feel like I must call my pediatrician every time my baby has a new rash, different-colored poop, or won't stop crying. How often should I be speaking with our doctor? How often is *too* often?

I used to work as a pediatric telephone triage nurse, and we would get all kinds of calls! It's absolutely okay to call your baby's doctor anytime you have a concern. That being said, I often suggest that parents take a deep breath and ask themselves, "Is this emergent or urgent?" Nine times out of ten, the answer will be "no." If your (older) baby has a fever, for instance, try managing it at home for a few hours and see what happens. If your baby won't get comfortable or is showing signs of dehydration, call in. Same goes for coughs and rashes. You can trust your gut and manage most things at home, and when you see that the condition is not improving or getting worse, that's a great time to call in. You may ask your doctor if they have a list of home treatment plans for common concerns so that you know exactly what they recommend and when they prefer you to call in.

Q. My friend had a baby around the same time I did, but her son is way ahead of mine developmentally. Should I be concerned? Am I doing something wrong?

No. Babies develop at different paces, and that's okay! Some have a "jump right in" personality and others have a "wait and watch" personality. I find that the babies who start hitting milestones earlier often do so with lots of falls and trial and error. They prefer to learn by doing, whereas babies who seem to be "late bloomers" are really just waiting until they are confident they will not fall or get hurt. I also find that "early birds" may have areas in which they may be lacking, and "late bloomers" may excel in another way. If your baby seems to be dramatically behind on many milestones, it may be worth a conversation with your provider.

Q. My baby loves to nurse to sleep and it makes my evening so easy but I was told it is a bad habit to be in and even advised that it could cause cavities when my baby develops teeth. Should I stop nursing my baby to sleep?

It is completely normal for breastfeeding to act as a sedative for your child. The hormones that are stimulated for both mother and baby during breastfeeding encourage sleep. Breastfeeding your baby to sleep is biologically normal and not a bad habit if it works for your family. Regarding concerns about breastfeeding and cavities, there is no data to support that breastfeeding causes cavities. Milk from the breast, due to the way the nipple is sucked to the back of the mouth, typically does not pool in the mouth as bottle-fed milk does. Ultimately, the introduction of complementary foods is more likely to cause cavities, so be sure to clean your baby's teeth before nursing to sleep, but you do not have to worry about waking your baby to clean their teeth after dream feeds.

Q. My breastfed baby's poop is green and mucousy; does that mean I should quit dairy?

Green and mucous-like stool can happen on occasion as a variation of normal. Sometimes it is an indication of inflamed bowels for one reason or another. One reason this could happen is if your baby is not receiving a proper balance of nutrition (for example, your baby isn't getting enough fatty milk). One recommended remedy to this problem would be ensuring that you are feeding the first breast to completion and offering the second as dessert. Sometimes for mothers with a fast letdown and oversupply of milk, this could require milk expression before feeding. Massaging the breasts before and during feeds can also help increase fat content in milk.

If your baby regularly experiences mucous-like stools with a foul odor, signs of blood, and pain, reach out to your health care provider for guidance.

Q. How do I pick the right car seat for my baby?

There are many things to consider when selecting a car seat for your baby. First and foremost, it is important to understand that all car seats are considered equally safe because they all have to meet the same testing standards. That said, some are easier to use properly than others and some car seats work better for different cars and different situations.

If you live in a city and primarily travel by taxi, you probably would consider using an infant carrier seat that can be installed quickly and easily with a seatbelt until your baby outgrows it. This is typically more convenient because the seat can simply click into a stroller as well for ease of use on sidewalks and subways. If you have your own vehicle, a convertible car seat may be a more economical option to grow with your baby. I recommend going to a store that has many car seats available and getting hands-on to see what you like best. Many stores will even let you take the seat to your car and see how well it installs and fits before you buy it. The Internet is a great resource, too. You can watch a lot of videos on installation techniques and safety, and find a certified child passenger safety technician (CPST) in your area for additional help.

Q. Should I be concerned about my baby spitting up and vomiting?

Spitting up can be within the realm of normal for a baby, especially if they are getting a lot of air when they feed or getting milk too quickly. Vomiting, however, can be something to watch closely. Projectile vomiting is different than forceful spit-up. Projectile vomiting will cover a pretty solid distance from where baby is stationary. If your baby is projectile vomiting, particularly as a newborn, you need to be seen by a care provider immediately. Remember to practice good hygiene during puke sessions, too. If baby has a stomach virus it can be contagious, so be mindful about washing your hands and sanitizing thoroughly once you get baby cleaned and settled. Otherwise, if your baby is a happy spitter and not in pain, you likely have more of a laundry problem than anything else.

Q. What is a tongue tie? Is it only a problem for breast-fed babies?

Tongue tie is the conversational term that refers to a thick band of tissue that prevents the tongue from functioning properly. This can impede feeding and speech and can contribute to a variety of conditions in your child. Most notably, babies with a tongue tie will be very uncomfortable and may have difficulty breastfeeding. However, breastfed babies are not the only babies who suffer from the complications of tongue ties, and bottle-feeding is not necessarily a solution to the problem. If you are concerned your baby has a tongue tie, regardless of your feeding choices, a lactation consultant knowledgeable in oral function and tongue tie can help you create a plan for treatment, which may include referrals to specialists.

Q. When can I start babywearing and how do I learn to do it safely?

Babywearing is a wonderful way to bond with your baby but can be very tricky to a newbie. I'll be honest, the first time I tried using a baby carrier I dropped my son. I caught him by his ankle before he hit the floor and I'm not sure I ever cried so hard or felt so scared and guilty. I swore off babywearing until I learned more. You can start wearing your baby as early as you want! You just have to make sure you have the appropriate carrier and are following proper safety protocols. Babywearing USA has babywearing groups around the United States that support learning more about babywearing. For a newborn, I recommend a ring-sling or wrap to provide the best support. Soft-structured carriers can be safe with inserts or following manufacturer recommendations. A postpartum doula or lactation consultant may also be able to help you. Other moms in your community are always a great resource as well.

If there just seem to be no options available for support, I recommend checking out YouTube. There are hundreds of tutorials on different kinds of carriers and how to use them. Once you figure it out, it will feel like second nature!

Q. I really need a break, but my baby is crying nonstop. I can't even set him down for a second and I feel like I'm ready to snap. What should I do?

Remember that crying is a way your baby communicates his needs. It can be frustrating when you aren't sure what they need, though. But it is important to remember your baby is NOT crying just to be difficult or to manipulate you. If your baby is fed, has a clean diaper, and is not showing signs of injury or illness, it is likely they just feel a need to connect. However, you can feel like you have done everything, and they still won't stop crying. If you are alone, take baby for a walk and see if fresh air helps them reset. If not, I recommend putting baby in a safe spot (like a playpen or crib) and walking outside by yourself for a few deep breaths and sunshine. Get a drink of water, go to the bathroom, and then go back to your baby and see if you can use your fresh mind to find a solution. If your baby is crying endlessly (for hours) it may be worth calling a friend or family member to come help you out and/or calling your baby's health care provider.

Q. I really feel like I do not want to be a parent anymore. I'm overwhelmed and struggling to cope with the demands. Even when I eat well, get exercise, and rest I feel tired all the time and like I can't keep up. What should I do?

First and foremost, I recommend that you call in your support system. Second, call your doctor. This could be the result of a health condition (nutritional deficiencies and hormone imbalances) or you could need a mental health referral to help manage postpartum depression or anxiety. I want you to know something very important, though. Parenting is hard. And you can do hard things. When you feel like you can't do hard things, that's a sign you need to call in the rest of your team. Although your baby is your responsibility, you were never meant to take on the responsibilities completely alone. We were designed to have social systems that support us, whether that's family or friends or community. Tap into those resources and do not allow embarrassment or fear to stop you from getting the support and love you deserve.

A Final Note

YAY! You did it! You made it through your baby's first year! Well... in the book, anyway! I hope by now you are feeling a little more prepared and confident to care for your baby. Even if there is nothing else you take away from this book, there are two things I need you to remember.

1. You are your baby's parent. Your instinct and your boundaries are trustworthy. You do not need to feel guilty for your limits, nor do you need to be embarrassed about your concerns. Your job is to raise a safe and healthy child. Your job is not to cater to society's demands.

2. Every family and every child's needs are different. The word *normal* is irrelevant. Do what is best for your family. Unless you are navigating medical conditions, your doctor's recommendations are merely that: recommendations. You're allowed to tailor advice to meet your family's needs. I'm so excited for your growing family and wish you all the best as you embark on this journey of welcoming your little bear!

FINAL PROMPT: *Go love on that brand-new baby of yours! These days may feel like forever but they certainly don't last that long. Enjoy your cuddly, curious little bear before toddlerhood kicks in and things get really interesting!*

Resources

Books:

- *Sweet Sleep* by La Leche League International
- *The Womanly Art of Breastfeeding* by La Leche League International

Websites:

- Feeding Support
  KellyMom.com
  MealTrain.com

- Find a lactation consultant:
  USLCA.org/resources/find-an-ibclc

- La Leche League International
  llli.org

- Postpartum Support International
  PostPartum.net
  Helpline: Call or text "Help" to 1-800-944-4773

- Women, Infants, and Children (WIC)
  WomenInfantsChildrenOffice.com

References

Castejón-Castejón, M., M. A. Murcia-González, J. L. Martínez Gil, J. Todri, M. Suárez Rancel, O. Lena, and R. Chillón-Martínez. "Effectiveness of Craniosacral Therapy in the Treatment of Infantile Colic: A Randomized Controlled Trial." *Complementary Therapies in Medicine* 47 (December 2019): 102164. doi:10.1016/j.ctim.2019.07.023.

Genna, Cathering Watson. "Breastfeeding and Perinatal Neuroscience." In *Supporting Sucking Skills in Breastfeeding Infants.* Burlington, MA: Jones & Bartlett Learning, 2017.

Gradisar, M., K. Jackson, N. J. Spurrier, J. Gibson, J. Whitham, A. S. Williams, R. Dolby, and D. J. Kennaway. "Behavioral Interventions for Infant Sleep Problems: A Randomized Controlled Trial." *PEDIATRICS* 137, no. 6 (June 2016): e20151486. doi:10.1542/peds.2015-1486.

La Leche League International. "The Safe Sleep Seven." November 28, 2018. llli.org/the-safe-sleep-seven.

Mindell, Jodi A., Brett R. Kuhn, and Daniel Lewin. "Behavioral Treatment of Bedtime Problems and Night Wakings in Infants and Young Children." *Sleep* 29, no. 10 (October 2006): 1263–76. doi:10.1093/sleep/29.10.1263.

UNICEF. "Co-Sleeping and SIDS: A Guide for Health Professionals." Last updated October 2019. UNICEF.org.uk /babyfriendly/wp-content/uploads/sites/2/2016/07 /Co-sleeping-and-SIDS-A-Guide-for-Health -Professionals.pdf.

Index

Normal, varieties of, 3, 145
Noses, cleaning, 90

O

Onesies, 97
Oral care, 90
Outings, 101–103, 105–106
Overwhelm, 8, 24, 142

P

Patience, 31–32
Pediatricians, 15, 137
Physical development, 81–82
Picking up babies, 26
Play, 100
Poop, 64, 70–72, 138–139
Postpartum depression, 5, 142

R

Rashes, 92
Reflexes, 82
Rest, importance of, 16, 60
Rompers, 98
Routines, bedtime, 58, 61–62

S

"Safe Sleep Seven" guidelines, 57
Safety
  bath, 77
  car seats, 102
  clothing, 98–99
  household, 14–15, 85
  sleep, 56–58
  solid foods, 52–53
  swaddling, 28–29
Sanctimommies, 4
Self-care, 6
Self-harm, thoughts of, 2
Senses, 82
Separation anxiety, 13, 104

Shushing, 31
Skin care. *See* Bathing
Skin irritation, 73, 92.
    See also Diaper rash
Sleep
  bedtime routines, 58, 61–62
  cries, 31
  importance of, 55
  needs, 55
  night waking, 61
  regressions, 59–60
  safety, 56–58
  training, 59
Sleepers, 97
Social development, 82
Social media, 5–6
Solid foods
  allergies, 52
  baby led weaning
    (BLW), 52–53
  choking hazards, 52–53
  introducing, 51
  readiness for, 50
  supplies, 50–51
Spitting up, 139–140
Stools (poop), 64, 70–72, 138–139
Strollers, 102
Sucking, 31
Sudden infant death
    syndrome (SIDS)
    prevention, 56–57
Support networks, 5, 15, 142
Swaddling, 27–29, 31
Swaying, 31

T

Teething, 90
Tongue tie, 140
Toys, 99–100

Acknowledgments

First, I'd like to give thanks to God for paving this path for me, opening doors I never knew existed, and showing me how to use my own challenging experiences for the good of others. I'd like to thank my husband, Sebastian, for being my rock during my own postpartum challenges, and supporting my desire to support other families who find themselves struggling like we did. Being a birth-worker's husband might be almost as stressful as being a military wife... *almost*. Thank you to my four Little Bears who have been my entire purpose and inspiration. Thank you to my parents for teaching me to be a fighter and to never give up. To Lydia and Taylor, thank you for letting me debrief not just birth-work, but life. To Nichole Joy for teaching me how to use my voice to reach and serve more families. Finally, thank you to the many families who have trusted me to help them navigate this very personal and special journey of becoming parents.

About the Author

 JAIMIE ZAKI is a military wife, homeschooling mother of four, licensed practical nurse, certified birth and postpartum doula, birth photographer, and international board certified lactation consultant (IBCLC). Jaimie owns and operates Little Bear Services, LLC, where she provides virtual (LittleBearLactation.com) and in-person support to new mothers during pregnancy and breastfeeding. Jaimie uses her own birth experiences combined with professional experiences to connect with and support families. Additionally, Jaimie helps families celebrate their own stories by using photography to document their journey into parenthood.